REA

ACPL ITEM
DISCARDED

Y0-BST-778

Get Over It!

EDUCATION REFORM IS DEAD.
NOW WHAT?

CAREN BLACK

ILLUSTRATIONS BY RICK CHARVET

HEINEMANN
Portsmouth, NH

Allen County Public Library

Heinemann
A division of Reed Elsevier Inc.
361 Hanover Street
Portsmouth, NH 03801–3912
www.heinemann.com

Offices and agents throughout the world

© 2002 by Caren Black

All rights reserved. No part of this book may be reproduced in any form or by any electronic or mechanical means, including information storage and retrieval systems, without permission in writing from the publisher, except by a reviewer, who may quote brief passages in a review.

The author and publisher wish to thank those who have generously given permission to reprint borrowed material:

Excerpt from *Left Back: A Century of Failed School Reforms* by Diane Ravitch is reprinted with the permission of Simon & Schuster Inc. Copyright © 2000 by Diane Ravitch.

Library of Congress Cataloging-in-Publication Data
Black, Caren.
  Get over it! : education reform is dead. now what? / by Caren Black ; illustrated by Rick Charvet.
    p. cm.
  Includes bibliographical references and index.
  ISBN 0-325-00281-9 (alk. paper)
  1. Education—United States. 2. Public schools—United States.
  3. Educational change—United States. I. Title.

LA217.2 .B57 2002
370'.973—dc21

2001051570

Editor: Lois Bridges
Production editor: Sonja S. Chapman
Cover design: Jenny Jensen Greenleaf
Typesetter: Tom Allen, Pear Graphic Design
Manufacturing: Steve Bernier

Printed in the United States of America on acid-free paper
06 05 04 03 02 VP 1 2 3 4 5

Contents

Acknowledgments

Many people in addition to the author put effort into the writing of a book. A huge round of applause and a big hug go to my incredibly talented, knowledgeable, and patient editor, Lois Bridges, for her always amazing ability to support a writer with glowing praise and still target the exact spots that need polishing. Working with her is an enormous privilege.

Heartfelt thanks to Rick Charvet, a truly gifted teacher, for a plethora of ideas and feedback, for "living the book" with me for the past two years, and for the invaluable contribution of his artwork.

Thanks to David Alsop of the Waldorf Schools Association North America and Michael Leahy, a member of American Montessori Internationale and founder of a Montessori middle school for the material they provided in interviews. Thanks to Suzanne Martino for her research efforts, and to Marc Sproule and Christopher Paddon for editing assistance.

Finally, thanks to all the friends who put up with and encouraged me! I hope you enjoy reading what you helped create!

Introduction

Hey! Thanks for the email. How was my day? Fairly routine:

8 A.M.: arrived at monthly safety meeting (we discuss things like gangs, graffiti, trends in illegal drug use, and security for upcoming student events). Got a cell call: 3 students caught leaving campus. Their backpacks were searched (routine for cuts). Found: a knife, a pipe, a rag, a lighter and some twine. The district safety officer and a police officer followed me back to campus. Turned out to be a meth pipe (with residue), a red bandana (gang "rag"), and a cigarette lighter. The twine was just twine. Oh, and a pocket knife with a 3" blade. Two suspensions, two arrests, two upset parents—all by 8:45 A.M.

8:55: A boy's mother called about another boy threatening her son. Got to the bottom of that one 8 boys later. Turns out Boy A was jumping up and down on a bench in the boys' locker room. Boy B told him to stop. Boy A didn't stop. Boy B got a group together after school and they approached Boy A. You get the picture.

    Told Boy B to let Boy A jump on the bench, that he was certain to get tired of it once it didn't bother Boy B any longer. Called in Boy A and asked him whether jumping on the bench was so much fun that it was worth risking getting in a fight and being suspended. He decid-

ed to stop jumping on the bench. Told him I thought that was a good plan.

9:34: Fire alarm went off. Real fire. Evacuated, but some kids assumed it was a drill and stood around. Some teachers stood around. Sent everyone out to the field. One boy tried to argue with me. Fire out. Checked in with the district and 911 and sent everyone back to class. On the way back, Girl A threw a nearly full can of soda at a garbage bin and Girl B got hit with it as she walked by. Finished dealing with Girl A and the kid who argued about the fire evacuation at 10:30.

    In between there were irate parents calling, wanting me to call the police because some kid said something to them or to their kid or both and they wanted to press charges. There was a girl who was tardy because she stayed with a friend all night after her dad locked her out of the house due to an argument she'd had with her mom. Then there was a boy who got sent out of class for putting a teacher's stuffed animals in compromising positions.

12:10: Lunch. Seven hundred pubescent kids with spring fever all eating outside. Fun talking with them. No injuries or incidents.

12:47: 12 kids in the office waiting for me and a report of another knife on campus. Had to let some of the kids go back to class because I had to search some backpacks for the knife. Took some time.

1:38 Report came in that a student has made a verbal threat against another student. The counselor and I

*called the two in. Finished with the backpacks (no knife)
and talked with one of the students. Threats earn a suspension—the fourth today.*

*2:11 School was almost over and a mother came to pick
up her child, saw another child she's angry with and
confronted the child in front of the school. Spoke with
her in my office and tried to resolve the issue. Informed
her about the Ed. Code regarding confronting other people's children on school property.*

*2:15 A parent picked up her child on the opposite side of
school and was upset with a student over there. Talked
with her as with the first parent. The bell rang and fully
one-half the office staff left for appointments I wasn't
told about earlier. Held down the fort. Finished some
paperwork and returned calls. Headed to my district
office meeting at 4:00, an hour late. Missed half of the
meeting, but managed to salvage a slice of pizza for
lunch. How was your day?* :-)

TTYL
CB

Like all descriptions in this book, this is a composite, and not
intended to resemble any actual person or event. Still, it's realistic.
Not all days are this eventful, but serving as Assistant Principal for
a middle school is a far cry from my work as director of a children's theatre company or as a consultant for small businesses in
planning, bookkeeping and taxes.

Part of my job has been to chair the local School Attendance
Review Board (SARB) working with parents and kids to help get

chronic truants back in school. Another part is to work with my district's alternative placements committee for students who are not succeeding in regular schools because of behavior, academic and attendance issues. I also work with local police, probation officers, restorative justice personnel, and community counselors. Well over 90% of the students I deal with are labeled seriously "at-risk," meaning their behavior and/or that of their parents jeopardizes their ability to graduate 8th grade, to stay out of jail, or potentially even to stay alive.

Often I don't feel much like an educator. I find it ironic that, with all my years of training and experience in music, drama, dance, education and business, a good deal of my job consists of police work—checking backpacks and pockets for drugs, weapons, or paraphernalia relating to drugs, gangs or graffiti. Nevertheless, I love working with the kids and, when I have the chance, working on curriculum and methods with teachers.

I loved all the years I was teaching. But, in my ten years in public education, I've been quite bothered by the number of programs that have come and gone, the good people that have done the same, and the feeling that keeping one's nose to the grindstone pays off with a stubby nose. I came from a different educational system, one where the payoff was always enormous satisfaction, growth and accomplishment—for me and for my students. I've kept looking for a way to recapture that in public education. I banked on education reform leading me there.

With a bachelor's degree in applied piano and a master's degree in theatre from Northwestern University; 20 years' dance training culminating with Chicago jazz dance master Gus Giordano; and with voracious reading in the ripe field of 60s–70s education theory and reform, I began my career as a performing arts teacher. I initiated a number of children's programs in music and drama, taught dance and creative movement for local park and rec programs in the East Bay area of Northern California, and managed two music schools for Yamaha International before opening my own school and children's repertory theatre company at the ripe old age of 27.

Subsequently I closed the school to work full time on the repertory company, wrote three original children's musicals and studied jazz dance with Rec Russell in Berkeley, applying my broad background with a degree of success that landed me in the pages of *Who's Who in California.* In Los Angeles I studied jazz dance with Joe Tremaine and began working for an independent production company at MGM/UA, a job that led to a ten-year detour through business.

When I decided to return to education in 1990, I chose public education rather than performing arts because of the current national publicity about reforms. Once again I immersed myself in reading: about education, education reform, alternative education, and about reforms in business and cultural thinking. I got involved. I wrote a design proposal for the New American Schools effort. I attended and presented at conferences, conventions and workshops. I earned teaching and administrative credentials and a language acquisition and development certificate.

I paid my dues. Several times. I originated projects, programs, a school within a school, authentic assessment tools, teacher guides. During the 90s, I talked with hundreds of educators, read over two hundred books on education, business, systems studies, human development, organizational development, the change process, ecology and future trends. I listened to business and lay people, scanned journals, participated in strategic planning, and took classes, always looking for the key that would make reforms stick. *How?* I repeatedly encountered the word *pendulum* but didn't then grasp its significance—only its recurrence.

Why, in public education, could I not feel the satisfaction I'd felt in the arts? Instead, I watched excellent new programs suffocate under the latest federal, state, or district focus. I learned that, despite the Herculean efforts of dedicated, intelligent people, things have a way of going back to where they were. Funding cuts, changes in administration, and simple short-sightedness extinguish new programs. One way or another, reforms seem to get buried under newer reforms and the result looks surprisingly like where we started.

Why?

I participated in and led districts' development of comprehensive new authentic assessments, rubrics, and curriculum standards. Over the ensuing years, I watched four districts repeat the same laborious process, oblivious to completed, tested, working models within 30 miles of them, unwilling to look or listen to what had already been done, and content to devour a year or two or more reinventing the wheel while kids and teachers waited.

Why?

Midway through the decade, I thought—as so many have—that the answer to my questions lay in the training and empowerment of teachers. I agreed with writer-speaker-teacher John Taylor Gatto: What we needed was a New Teacher, one firmly grounded in pedagogical and brain theory, experienced in some "real world" occupation outside education, empowered to make major decisions regarding program and placement, and paid accordingly.

My master's project in administration, "Pedagogy of the New Teacher," provided a vehicle for working with teachers where I taught and became the basis of my book *Getting Out of Line: A Guide for Teachers Redefining Themselves and Their Profession*. In it, I wrote, "We cannot begin to believe in the potential of every student until we believe in the potential of every teacher" (1997, 34). I truly believed in teachers' ability to turn things around and was determined to use any administrative position I attained to help them do just that. It took only one year as an administrator to realize that my chosen key could not unlock reform in public education.

Why?

The question plagued me. If teachers were not the key, then what *was*? Why couldn't a cadre of teacher leaders at each site make a difference? One reason seemed to be the strata of isolation in public education. Administrators see themselves as separate from teachers; teachers see themselves as separate from students; politicians see themselves as separate from everybody and seem to focus mainly on getting elected to the next higher office (safely out of the picture by the time the side effects of their short-sighted legislation are felt).

More than that, people's individual specialized roles isolate them. Teachers, students, parents, politicians, higher education, textbook, test, and software publishers, administrators, support staffs, business, communities, and service agencies all see the education process from their disparate self-interests. Amazingly, their views rarely coincide, let alone overlap, and often collide. Teachers can't be "key" when so many remote factions are involved. The pieces we ignored were killing the pieces we reformed.

Then there's the lack of genuine risk-taking. Typical of the generalized fear that comes with working in an addictive organization (Schaef and Fassel 1988), many teachers don't want the responsibility that comes with autonomy and empowerment. Symbiotically, most people who make policy for teachers—unions, administrators, boards, and legislatures—don't want to give it to them anyway.

So, where is the focus for reform, if not on teachers? If reforms seem always to focus on isolated areas and fail because of all the *other* interdependent areas not taken into consideration, how do we develop a coherent picture of the whole with all its interrelating parts? If it was what we each didn't know about the other parts coupled with lack of empowered and enlightened teachers that seemed to be killing reforms, could we overcome these obstacles to bring about efficient, effective and lasting change?

The seeds of this book germinated in the conviction that we could. If a book could explain our education system *as a whole*, if it could illustrate the big picture of how the disparate parts directly and indirectly affect each other, readers could make better, more informed choices. In the performing arts, I was used to "translating" among musicians, actors and dancers who work in similarly separated fields. With my added experience in business and writing, I felt I might have the requisite tools to help translate once again. I could write a germinal systems study and we could begin to propose reforms that could actually be sustained.

But, *could we*?

Could we each see outside our limited perspectives? Until a recent influx of mid-lifers choosing a second career, most educators seemed to have little experience in any other field, having entered teaching straight from college. Many come from families of educators, with a parent teaching or an uncle in administration, or someone on the school board. A fish that has never leapt out of the water has no concept of water. Water is only *reality* or *the way things are*. Therefore, water is *assumed* and unchangeable at any fundamental level. In other words, thinking out of the box requires leaving the box in order to even see that one is, in fact, in a box in the first place.

While many teachers' lives have entirely centered on public education both as students and as teachers, few legislators have classroom teaching experience. Parents cover a wide spectrum of experience, but have little knowledge of the day-to-day classroom or of the laws and regulations governing public education. Test and text publishers must bow to their bottom line. Unions have their own specific agendas. Bus drivers and custodians have theirs. Colleges, theirs. While it had become apparent to me that the provincial nature of our individual efforts kept reforms from succeeding, it was becoming equally obvious that we might lack the means to correct this gargantuan tangle.

Why?

The more materials I gathered for my systemic illustration, the more complex my task became. After numerous false starts, I still lacked a clear systemic model until I read *The Web of Life: A New Scientific Understanding of Living Systems* by Fritjof Capra. There I found the fertile ground I needed to answer all my *Why?* questions and to inform my writing.

This book is my attempt to share what I've learned. In it, the reader will find a path, not a recipe. You will be asked to draw on your own experience and to take a fresh, unconventional look at other forms of education right in your own backyard. You'll be coaxed to look at current public education as *one form* of reality, rather than the only possibility. Never fear—I will not use that bludgeoned and bloody term, *paradigm shift.* We won't get quite that far, but we're en route.

You will find no step-by-step directions for how to set up a new school or design a new school system, though I know many educators would like just that. In Los Angeles at the New American Schools Design Conference (NASDC) workshop in 1991, about half the attendees were from business, half from education. The panel presented their request for proposals (RFP) and their rationale and requirements for grants. Then they opened two floor mics for people who wanted to ask questions.

People who introduced themselves as members of the business world tended to ask questions like, "You mean we could design a school on a bus?" Yes. "Would you consider schools using offsite instructors—distance learning?" Yes. "Could we have schools where professionals—experts—give master classes?" Yes. Educators' questions included, "How many pages does the proposal have to be?" (This was asked several times.) And, "Do you want the proposal double-spaced?"

Educators in general tend to like recipes. Curriculum-in-the-Box. Overall, we're not risk takers. It's been beaten out of us. This book will help us understand why.

A respected teacher sat in my office midyear discussing the fact that he'd addressed only one-tenth of the state framework in the first semester and and his plan for second semester would address only another tenth. He was reluctant, however, to deal with the other 80% of what he'd been hired to teach because he didn't like to try anything new until he was "110% sure" of how it would come out. For that he needed summer planning time. It mattered little what subject he was teaching or how many concepts he covered, he embodied the underlying subliminal message to students that it's better to not try at all than to try and possibly fail.

Teachers like this one need more than permission to fail. We need to hide their recipes and help them trust themselves so they can teach their students to do the same. This particular teacher ended up trying something new with my guidance, experienced great success with it and was quite pleased with the techniques and tools he gained. But he had *permission* to try and someone who believed in him. Even that didn't feel like enough to him at first, though it turned out to be more than sufficient.

This book is about permission to try, not recipes for doing. It's about belief in oneself. My editor calls it "a polemic, rather than a how-to." She's a very smart lady. I do attack conventional assumptions. Other sources? I can offer few to none inside The Box of public education, for The Box is firmly closed and the current rhetoric of change takes place *within* it. I ask the reader to first notice The Box, then dare to step outside. I require transfer and application of concepts and models from other fields.

I present four major concepts:

1. Education is a closed system
2. Closed systems preclude reform
3. Open learning systems exist which could be used as models
4. Parallel public systems could exist to everyone's benefit.

Each of these concepts could consume a hundred pages in explanation, but what would be the point? Aside from the obvious fact that nonfiction of four or five hundred pages is costly and not reader-friendly, no self-empowerment volume is thick enough to satisfy the recipe contingent or those who prefer to rearrange the deck furniture on the Titanic, insisting the boat is a perfectly safe miracle of modern science. People do not benefit from more explanation when it's not what they want to hear in the first place.

On the other hand, as every teacher knows whose students are ready for the concepts presented, a word to the wise is sufficient. These people apply information in ways we never dream of. It's hard to stop them; they take the information and run with it, improve and expand upon it, make it their own. They do not need the details filled in for them.

Years ago, one of my dearest students went with his family to see the musical, *A Chorus Line*. He was ten, and he embarrassed his parents by giggling all through the song that repeats the word *gonorrhea*. Driving home, thinking of ways to broach the subject, his mother asked whether he'd enjoyed the musical. "Oh, yes!" he enthused, "Especially the part about that guy who had diarrhea!" We take that for which we are ready.

Conversely, in the 70s, during a speech in San Francisco, Gloria Steinem said that a raised consciousness is a one-way door;

once through, one cannot go back. It's equally true that we tend not to even approach the door until we're ready or we are propelled there. Up to that point, we take only what fits into our current frame. There's an old joke that housecats watch sadly as we drive away in the morning, not because they'll miss us, but because they feel sorry for us. From their perspective, getting into a car means going to that place where people wear white coats and take one's temperature rectally. Anais Nin put it this way: "We don't see the world as it is. We see it as we are" (Schiller 1999).

So now, if you are ready, the ensuing pages will lead you outside the current frame of public education and into a potential future. This book is, to use a zen phrase, only a finger pointing at the moon. The finger is not the moon and cannot bring it down from the sky (Winokur 1989). The book points at a solution, but is not the solution itself. The solution lies within the readers as much as the writer.

> Out of discussion we call to vision,
> to those desiring to see we point the path;
> our teaching is a guiding in the way;
> the seeing must be the very act of him who has made the choice.
> —PLOTINUS (Schiller 1999)

1

Where Are We?

"Toto, I don't think we're in Kansas anymore. . . ."
—DOROTHY, IN *THE WIZARD OF OZ*

Just where *are* we in the process of reforming public education today? We started out down a yellow brick path with expectations similar to Dorothy and friends. Have we arrived at Oz yet? Maybe we have. That could be the problem.

In the past quarter century, what has been done? Hundreds of books have been written on education reform. In California alone (America's largest school system), thousands of laws have been passed and hundreds of billions of dollars spent. Nearly all other states have consistently spent more per pupil. Nationally, education spending has increased between 61% and 100% over the last 25 years, depending on the index used (Bracey 1997, 29). It stands to reason that all this effort must have accomplished a great deal. If *Kansas* is where we started, surely Dorothy is correct and we can't be in that state anymore.

Then I repeat: Where are we? What state are we in?

Some might say we're in the state of exhaustion with a nagging feeling that education should be reformED by now. Each new

1

package, method, focus area leaves us a little more disinterested, disheartened, disenchanted than the last. Many of us have developed skepticism about the ability of brand new reforms to do anything at all. Conversely, many of us *continue* to work feverishly on reform efforts, convinced that things *are* somehow different, better, or that this new legislation, that new funding source, this new reading program, that new textbook series, this new teacher training program, that accountability package, new incentive program or standardized test will somehow make a big difference.

But will it? Given all that's already been done in the past twenty-five years, what are the odds?

We are infatuated with statistics, but they are not altogether kind. Since 1975, combined SAT scores have declined (Bracey 1997, 53). The number of high school dropouts has increased by 38,000 even though the number of seventeen-year-olds has decreased by 324,000 (NCES 1999, table 104)! Forty percent of teenaged girls become pregnant at least once, giving the U.S. the highest rate of teen pregnancy in the western industrialized world and costing around $7 billion annually. Only 33% of teen mothers receive a high school diploma (compared with 71% of teens overall) and their children tend to do poorly in school (NCPTP 2000, 1–2).

Kids wear society's problems to school and we don't like the fashion statement.

So, politicians make education reform one of their major goals. The press carries complaints that Americans are increasingly illiterate. High-tech businesses complain that entry-level American workers lack adequate basic skills to compete in the world market. Legislators pass literally hundreds of education laws annually in California alone, yet the complaints keep coming.

In short, we seem to have done one heck of a lot of complaining, explaining, reforming, spending and general noisemaking without quite the desired effect. Many of us continue to follow our yellow brick road of reform, investing our hopes in each new effort like Dorothy and friends hoping for the Wizard's answers to their problems—with much the same result.

Why? Why have so many well intentioned people spent so much time and money and effort over such an extended period and achieved so little, proportionately, in return? How could that possibly be? Surely the results must be there somewhere! Surely we've made some progress, but the *conditions* have continued to get more difficult. Surely if we could just measure our results better, get better teachers, coerce students into doing their homework, involve parents more. . . . If there were more money, more time, more of *something.* . . . If we could only figure out exactly what that something is! Wouldn't it work *then*?

There's a simple answer: Nope.

"Why *not*?" you protest. "That's ridiculous! *Something* has to work." No, it doesn't. Not the way we've been going about it, at least. You see, no matter how many pigs you throw off a roof, you're never going to get one of them to fly. Pigs don't, you know. They do lots of other useful things, though—those are the things you need to concentrate on with pigs, not flight. If it's flight you really want, you need to let the pigs go and get yourself something with wings. Or, maybe you need to let the pigs do what pigs do best and add your flight element with something else. Maybe you need choice. Or maybe you just need to stop throwing things off the roof.

Einstein put it something like this: "The problems we have created at the level of thinking we have done thus far cannot be solved at that same level of thinking." He knew about the pigs.

The point is, *what we don't know about our education system threatens what we do know.* There are very concrete reasons why reform—as we've tried it—has not worked. And why it won't. Ever. But, there are other things that *can.* To *reform* is literally to form/create/shape something again; commonly it means to amend or improve. If you believe that *either* meaning applies to what we're doing in public education, then this is your "warning label": Some content that follows may cause headache or nausea; some of what is described may not seem suitable for young children.

Where's the problem? The people who've been involved in education reform are no dummies. They're educated, well intentioned people, usually quite committed to the cause. What then gives me the temerity to say we're following some yellow brick road or will succeed only when pigs fly? Two reasons: *syllabification* and *old information.*

First, syllabification: We have, as my high school English teacher used to say, "Put the em-PHAS-is on the wrong syl-LA-ble." In fact, we've been so invested in syllabification that we've lost the entirety of the word. Hardly anyone is looking at the big picture. John Godfrey Saxe's poem is worth rereading:

The Blind Men and the Elephant

It was six men of Indostan to learning much inclined,
Who went to see the elephant (Though all of them were
    blind),
That each by observation might satisfy his mind.

The first approached the elephant, and, happening to fall
Against his broad and sturdy side at once began to bawl:
"Why, bless me! but the elephant is very like a wall!"

The second feeling of the tusk, cried: "Ho! what have we
    here,
So very round, and smooth, and sharp? To me 'tis very
    clear,
This wonder of an elephant is very like a spear!"

The third approached the animal, and, happening to take
The squirming trunk within his hands, thus boldly up he
    spake:
"I see," quoth he, "the elephant is very like a snake!"

The fourth reached out his eager hand, and felt about the
    knee:
"What most this wondrous beast is like, is very plain,"
    quoth he:
"'Tis clear enough the elephant is very like a tree!"

The fifth, who chanced to touch the ear, said: "E'en the
    blindest man
Can tell what this resembles most; deny the fact who can,
This marvel of an elephant is very like a fan!"

The sixth no sooner had begun about the beast to grope,
Then, seizing on the swinging tail that fell within his scope,
"I see," quoth he, "the elephant is very like a rope!"

And so these men of Indostan disputed loud and long,
Each in his own opinion exceeding stiff and strong;
Though each was partly in the right, and all were in the
    wrong.
[emphasis added]

"The Blind Men and the Elephant" is an apt analogy for public education reformers because we've been blinded by isolation and lack the perspective of systems design. From teachers teaching in isolated classrooms to curricular frameworks being written for each subject area by completely separate groups of people, all the way to legislators creating statutes without stepping foot in a classroom, we prod, grope, seize and dispute without any overarching perspective of what's truly possible. As a result, each person or

Figure 1–1
Education Elephant

group acts in good conscience and with the best of intent, though each is "partly in the right, and all [are] in the wrong."

We must look at the big picture, but that is only the beginning. We need new information on what makes our elephant tick, about what it's capable of doing and what it cannot do. Just as a pig's design precludes flight, our elephant, too, has its limitations.

We must examine what about the current system's design has contributed to the failure of reform efforts. We need to check out other systems' designs currently in use and to imagine brand new system designs based on twenty-first century systems thinking. We need to plot our escape from The Box.

2

Box? What Box?

Normally, we do not so much look at things as overlook them.

— ALAN WATTS (Schiller 1999)

As part of my research, I asked administrators, teachers, and friends outside education to describe our public education system, making it clear that I was requesting a picture of The Box, not a critique of it. Several admitted that it was far more difficult to write description than criticism, but all tried, and I am grateful for their efforts. The result: 43 responses, including metaphors such as *a train in motion* and *a melting pot*. Only one tackled the actual systemic structure. That is, only one attempted to describe The Box itself. Again, we are so immersed in our current system that we have trouble seeing it.

In her book, *Left Back: A Century of Failed School Reforms*, Diane Ravitch quotes William C. Bagley, a national education leader in the 30s, on school reforms:

> Bagley insisted that there were no shortcuts to improvement of the schools. No country in the world, he says, had witnessed so many educational reforms in the past generation as the United

States: "It has been one nostrum after another." To make matters worse, the schools had developed a huge top-heavy bureaucracy, with the teacher at the bottom of the heap. None of this made much difference, he said. The fundamental factor in education was the quality of classroom teachers. (2000, 290–291)

However we view—or ignore—the system itself, it is still true that we aim our reform efforts at the part with which we are most familiar, the classroom, i.e., teachers, students, books, methods. This is a fatal error. As Bagley pointed out, the classroom is inconsequential as the system is set up. "What do you mean 'The classroom is inconsequential'? That's ridiculous! The classroom is where education takes place!" Ridiculous? True—but hold that thought.

The public education system is, of course, a hierarchical bureaucracy. Its multiple layers begin at the highest level with the federal government and continue down at least four more levels and laterally across three to eight agencies per level until they reach the bottom of the heap: the classroom. (See Figure 2–1, p. 10.) "Wait a minute," you say. "That's not how I'd describe it!" My point, exactly. Yet there it is.

We have an Industrial Age, hierarchical bureaucracy with what *should* be the governing piece—the teacher's classroom—placed instead at the bottom of the chain of command. This should be our first clue as to why our best intended efforts have not produced what we thought they would.

Industrial Age factories were our model. But, 80s business reformer W. Edwards Deming and others showed business that you can fire all the workers on a factory assembly line and replace them with different ones. It won't increase the efficiency of the factory by any significant margin or over any significant time span. In fact, over time, the efficiency with the second set of workers, if it increased at all, will tend to return to the same level it was with the first set.

Figure 2–1
Education Hierarchy Flow Chart

In education this is the pendulum effect.

Much has been written about our system's factory model, assembly line structure. Since the Industrial Age, we've passed the Atomic Age and entered the Information Age, but our system, like most government bureaucracies, maintains a design nearly two centuries old. It's like trying to prepare someone to navigate cyberspace by training them to steer a Model T. The design is out of synch with the times, with what we're trying to do in education today, with the population we're educating.

Let's examine our Industrial Age system by comparing it to something mechanical, as befits its age of origin. James Watt's centrifugal governor for the steam engine is often used as an example of a self-regulating mechanical system. In the steam engine governor, when pressure builds up, speed of rotation increases. The increased speed combines with centrifugal force to raise small hanging weights attached to a valve. As these weights rise, they cause the valve to open and release the pressure. With released pressure, speed decreases, centrifugal force decreases, and the weights lower, closing the valve. The cycle repeats, keeping the pressure fairly constant, or in equilibrium.

This self-regulating cycle is called a *feedback loop*. The example of the centrifugal governor was often used by Norbert Wiener, one of the pioneers of cybernetics. Feedback is common in both mechanical and living systems. A mechanical system like the centrifugal governor—one that operates near *equilibrium*, back and forth, open/closed—is called a *closed system*. The tendency in a closed system is toward equilibrium: to return to center, to remain the same (Capra 1996, 56–61). Due to the pervasive influence of Newtonian physics and its "clockworks" view of the universe, nearly everything in our contemporary world has been viewed as a mechanical system, including us.

A rubber band provides a simple visual metaphor. A rubber band stretches to accommodate objects, but the tension that holds those objects (making the rubber band useful) is created by the *tendency of the band to return to its original shape*. This tendency, in fact, holds its value, makes it work. For example, we bundle—or rubber band—a group of reform packages. We stretch the band to accommodate extra reading time, incorporate spelling, develop students' decoding of math story problems, and deal with one or two indigenous site or district issues. This stretching creates tension and the urge to *return to our original form*, possibly even to the point of teachers closing the classroom door and doing just that. *The value of a closed system lies in the tendency to remain the same.*

The pendulum effect finally begins to make sense on a much deeper level. "Never throw out materials from an old method. Just wait long enough and they'll come back." Phonics and sight recognition, skill/drill and manipulatives, vocational education and algebra for everyone, the arts and the "Three Rs"—all have been included, excluded, and included again. So have small schools, large schools, and the breaking down of large schools into small schools within the large school.

As a working hypothesis, let's equate equilibrium in our school system with acceptable test scores, since they seem to be what we still accept, albeit grudgingly, as a standard measure of how we're doing. The center or equilibrium point we keep working toward would then be good test scores across the board—all students, all subject areas.

When scores are low in reading and writing, we would thus make a correction, or self-regulate, by concentrating efforts on language arts. We'd adopt new texts and materials, change requirements, add teacher training, add specialists and consultants, allocate specially earmarked funds and demand accountability. When reading scores begin to show improvement—to return to equilibrium—we'd look at math scores, which may have fallen during our focus on reading, and begin the fix-it process on them. While we're concentrating on math, reading scores may slide again. Back and forth, back and forth goes the pendulum, crossing the center twice as often as any other point.

Capra's description of closed systems and living systems in *The Web of Life* throws our oft-quoted pendulum metaphor into bold relief, answering my first question, Why? Why could Diane Ravitch fill 467 pages with the highlights of a century of failed reforms? Why haven't we passed out of our Reformation and into our Renaissance? The answer is, *We can't help it. The system is designed that way.*

A pendulum is like a closed system. In its own way, it self-corrects, each extreme causing it to reverse direction toward the opposite extreme. It always attempts to return to the center, to equilibrium. This is its function. Reform efforts in a closed system are a little like teaching a pig to sing—don't try. It's a waste of time, and it annoys the pig.

In this light, *not one school reform has ever failed*! They've all worked perfectly according to the system they're in. They take over for a moment, then return to center.

Therefore, what we need is not better reforms, but a different system, one that accepts and assimilates reform. Does such a system exist? Yes. You are one.

Ludwig von Bertalanffy wrote in *General System Theory* (1968) that there are "open systems," which operate in a state far from equilibrium "characterized by continual flow and change" (Capra 1996, 48). Living systems, like you, are open systems. To study them, we must move from our Newtonian mechanical physics view of the universe to Einsteinian relativity and quantum physics. We must move from ideas of independence and dominance to interdependence, from entropy to transformation.

Von Bertalanffy speculated that classical science would have to be supplemented by new theories that would incorporate these living systems. In the 1970s, Ilya Prigogine applied new developments in mathematics to do just that. The state of continually operating far from equilibrium is known as a *steady state* and allows not only change and growth, but *evolution* (Capra 1996, 48–49). That is, it not only accepts and assimilates change within the system, but also allows change to the system itself. *The value of an open system lies in its ability to adapt, evolve, grow—to change.*

Next, we'll use one California reform, Class Size Reduction, as an example of how our focusing on the bottom rung in the hierarchy, our ignoring the big picture of interrelated pieces, and our system's very design all contributed to reducing this reform's effectiveness.

3

Class Size Reduction
An Example of Major School Reform

To fall into habit is to cease to be.
                    —MIGUEL DE UNAMUNO (Schiller 1999)

To boost academic achievement, Californians have tried to put fewer students in each class (SB1777, 1996). This seemed like a logical, admirable reform for the nation's largest K–12 system. Fewer students to each teacher—one third fewer—should give the teacher more time with each individual student. More teacher time should equal better education.

The average class size, kindergarten through eighth grade, in the U.S. in 1995–96 was 17.1. California's was 24.1, the highest in the nation (EdSource 1997–98, 19). For Class Size Reduction reform, California chose 20, kindergarten through third grade, as Tennessee had done, when habits and patterns get established and when kids are learning to read, seemingly a reasonable age.

Senator Jack O'Connell introduced the bill in the California Senate. By the time Governor Pete Wilson signed it July 15,1996, the public, the press, and the politicians all seemed to feel that this was a reform that would make a significant difference. California's Class Size Reduction (CSR) program was "the largest state educational reform in history . . . [costing] over 1.5 billion per year and [affecting] over 1.8 million students" (CSR Research Consortium, 2000, 3). CSR became the new hope, the reform that would make all the other reforms work. The thinking was that the problem all along had been too many kids per teacher.

Quality of instruction *is* affected by class size, to be sure. In what way it's affected depends on a variety of factors. If the subject is square dancing, it's entirely possible for two people to teach 200, given a ballroom with a stage and a sound system. With a large group, participants can do more in terms of lines and changing partners and dancing in a square—and may have a lot more fun than in a private lesson.

The optimum student-teacher ratio depends on three primary factors, as we shall see. If we're learning how to divide fractions by inverting and multiplying, one teacher can serve somewhere between one and 60 students, depending on the strength of the teacher and the ability level(s) of the student(s). If it's polishing the second movement of a Beethoven sonata or perfecting a tennis serve or editing a piece of writing, one-on-one instruction is often essential, certainly no more than one-to-four or one-to-five. If improving "text decoding" (reading) is the object, between one and five students with one very good teacher can accomplish a lot.

Learning a new language, how to play soccer, how to factor an equation, how to write an essay, how to make an outline, effective ways to make a speech, how to form a precipitate, complete an electrical circuit, design a chip, write a program, operate a computer, service a transmission, administer CPR, apply for a job, take standardized tests, add, multiply, speak a second language . . . The implications are as obvious as the tasks are different.

I've watched one teacher hold 60 first graders in rapt attention and one teacher with an aide struggle to maintain the focus of twelve. In strictly pedagogical terms, the number of students it's possible to educate well is directly related to:

- subject matter
- purpose of instruction
- expertise of teacher and student(s)

When one of these factors changes, the optimal size varies.

Does smaller class size insure better education? Clearly, the answer is, "That *depends*." Yet, within The Box of public education, school is a continuous (assembly) line of classes of one standard size, in one standard type of room, in one standard configuration with other rooms, under standard rules and regulations with one standardized (credentialed) teacher. Our bureaucratic system likes yes/no answers. Back/forth, open/closed, standardization. Simple, neat, easy to deal with. However, *that depends* or *it varies* are more complex and require broader thinking. They don't fit inside The Box.

For the CSR reform, we once again:

- aimed at the weakest point in the chain of command—the classroom—while leaving unchecked the powers that govern that link.
- assumed that class size is the keystone for academic success.
- ignored the bigger picture with its symbiotic factors like facility and teacher shortage.
- discounted the pendulum effect, which could increase class size again at a downturn in the economy (or some other variable).

In short, CSR is another inside-the-box reform, or reform-in-the-box.

The effects?

The academic effects of class size do not operate independently from other factors. Take teachers, for example. Cutting average class size from 30-something down to 20 means that 60 students who were using two classrooms and two teachers now require three of each. Because there has been a simultaneous shortage of both teachers and facilities, CSR means we now have 20 students remaining in room A with teacher A, 20 in room B with teacher B, and 20 in a former janitor's storage closet with a teacher whose two strongest qualifications may be a pulse and an emergency credential.

While CSR was making untrained teachers a major problem for California, the state cut back on staff training days in order to increase student attendance days. Students in one-fourth of the grades were in smaller classes. The result? The entire system felt the effects of fewer credentialed teachers. There was less training time for all teachers. Materials and facilities became completely inadequate. When the pendulum is forced in one direction, it will naturally traverse an equal path in the opposite direction.

While CSR was aimed at grades K–3, it impacted grades four and up both positively and negatively. The intent is that after three or four years in smaller classes, by the time students get to sixth grade they will continue to do better there, too, even in a larger class. However, many veteran teachers in upper grades took a look at what they deemed a one-third workload reduction, exercised their seniority and transferred to a primary grade. Now we have veteran sixth-grade teachers teaching second grade, harmless enough but perhaps not an improvement. This, in turn, left the sixth grade class not only with thirty-plus students, but often with a newly hired, emergency-credentialed teacher.

Ask a teacher. One of the most challenging aspects of teaching is finding ways to reduce whole-class instruction time. Whole-class instruction is overwhelmingly direct instruction. This type of teaching is most effective for relaying information, setting up activities, and brief reviewing. Small groups or individual work is pedagogically preferred for many subjects and skills, including math practice, experiments, and reading.

The CSR Research Consortium reports that in Language Arts (reading and writing) in reduced-size classes, the average number of minutes of whole class instruction actually went up 34% in 1998–99 over 1997–98 (2000, 10). This could be related to the increased number of inexperienced teachers. "Clearly class size reduction in and of itself is only part of the story" (EdSource February 1998, 4) The causes are interdependent. The result is less effective teaching.

Following CSR, new materials were required to set up thirty-three percent more classrooms in the primary grades and equip those new teachers. Intermediate grades might have to do without or postpone equipment expenditures. Wasn't CSR funded by the state? Yes. $11 billion the first year. $650 was provided per student for every class of twenty in 1996–97 and $800, or $1.273 billion in 1997–98 (Molnar 2000, 50; EdSource 1998–99, 7). In 1998-99 approximately $1.5 billion went to kindergarten through third grades and another $80 million toward ninth grade. In 1996, shortfalls amounted to about $125 per student (WestEd 1996). That's nearly $120 million that districts had to come up with from budgets already ranked forty-first in the nation in 1996 for per-pupil expenditures (EdSource November 1998, 1). Equipment and supplies were bound to suffer.

CSR turned a facilities problem into an emergency. Portable classroom manufacturers ran out of stock. Rooms never intended as classrooms were pressed into service. Creativity reigned—like four classes sharing two rooms, traveling among classroom, library and playground all day so that each class could get some time in an actual classroom. "Both nationally and here in California, government leaders and educators agree that the problem of school facilities has reached crisis proportions. . . . Moreover, this circumstance constrains the ability of many schools to improve public education through such measures as class size reduction . . ." (EdSource April 1998, 1). By 1999, fully one-third of the classrooms in California's 8000 schools are portables (Dannis 1999).

The academic year 1996–97 saw 955,333 California primary students enter reduced-size classrooms (EdSource 1997–98, 7). By the end of the third year of CSR (1998–99), 1.8 million of California's six million students were in reduced-size classes (CSR Research Consortium 2000, 4). The results so far? "Not so clear—and may not be for at least five years (2002)—is what impact [this] will have on public education as a whole" (EdSource February 1998, 1). Evaluation models were begun after the program started, so there will be no comparable preprogram data.

Tennessee's program had built-in data collection from inception. And? "Overall, the results were somewhat mixed" (EdSource February 1998, 4). In an Austin, Texas trial, ten schools "showed little or no improvement in student achievement" (EdSource February 1998, 4). Other sources, citing research from Tennessee, Wisconsin, and Nevada, disagree: "There is no longer any argument about whether reducing class size in the primary grades increases student achievement. The research evidence is quite clear: It does" (Molnar 2000, 53). The press is not convinced: "Smaller classes could be one of the most important school reforms in recent years—or a colossal waste of money" (EdSource February 1998, 8). According to a California League of Middle Schools legislative committee meeting in Sacramento in the winter of 2001, the new Governor's office seems to be giving out the message that Class Size Reduction doesn't work and therefore isn't to be considered among middle school reforms. And this pig had a cape and everything! What happened?

Figure 3–1
Throwing Pigs Off the Roof Again

Whichever side of the debate one personally favors is really irrelevant. The intended benefits obviously cannot all have been lost. Teachers report favorably on their ability to interact personally with each student in a twenty-student class. The degree to which the unintended complications dilute the benefits will vary from year to year, class to class. But CSR will not "save" public education in California—or anywhere else for that matter—nor will it have a huge effect over time. We ignored both the big picture *and* the system's inevitable return to equilibrium. Now what?

4

Now What?

*The real voyage of discovery consists not in seeking new
landscapes, but in having new eyes.*
—MARCEL PROUST (Schiller 1999)

At an education conference a few years ago, I picked up a
button at an ecology exhibit. It reads, "If you're not out-
raged, you're not paying attention." Many readers may be
feeling something akin to outrage at this point:

> Great. So you're saying nothing will work. Reform isn't possible.
> The system "precludes" it. That's really positive, really helpful. I
> can almost do something with that on Monday morning. Don't
> you find anything *good* about public education? Any successes?
> Well, your system may "preclude" reform, lady, but I'm still
> going to keep trying to make my system work better, because it's
> the only one I've got!

Actually, it isn't. There are systems of education which have
existed for centuries, well before public education was legislated in
this country, well before this country was founded. But, we'll need
new eyes with which to examine them because they are all but

invisible from inside The Box. There are also private academic systems developed during the 20th century in Europe which are thriving in the United States. We'll take a look at the design of two of those systems. Finally, there are "doors" in our current system, potential ways out of The Box, that could become an open, *living* system. True, nothing will be in place this Monday morning. Finding a way out of The Box demands real change. No recipes. No quick fixes. A lasting, substantive transformation is different from the familiar quick fix, but it doesn't have to take a long time, either. The models are right under our noses, just waiting for creative, intelligent educators, parents and policy makers to wake up and smell the coffee.

Artistic and Athletic Coaching Models

Follow along an icy sidewalk on the near North side of Chicago. The January winds blowing in off Lake Michigan create a chill factor of thirty degrees below zero on this Saturday morning. We have a seven-block walk with Diedra to catch the "L" to Evanston. Approaching the station, we see the wheels spark as a train screams in. The steps up to the platform are covered with lumps of brown snow, frosted over during the night. Clapping our hands together to stay warm, we catch our train. At the Davis Street station, we reverse the process, exiting the station steps and walking four more blocks and up two flights of stairs to the studio. We have just enough time to get out of our ton of coats and scarves and boots, thaw out, and begin warmups—aptly named, but put to the test this frigid morning.

Diedra was given her Christmas wish: Her single mom saved up enough money for her to take dance lessons at a professional studio in Evanston. She is on her way to audition for ballet class, which is recommended training before studying her first love: hip-hop and jazz dance. She is twelve and would like to become a professional dancer. For the past three and a half years she's studied at a small studio two blocks from her apartment, but her teacher told her mother that the most advanced classes there are no longer challenging enough. The girl has talent and should move on. Depending on Diedra's audition, she will be placed in either the preteen or the more advanced teen class; the very top students take class with the adults. She is hoping that the practice she has done on her own will qualify her for the teen class.

Inside the classroom studio, students are milling about, talking and laughing quietly, some stretching at the barre or on the floor, others finishing with the tying on of shoes and the securing of warmup leggings and sweaters. All the girls, except those with short hair, wear crocheted bun covers over their neatly secured tresses. Diedra's tight curls aren't long enough for a bun, but she's made sure they are pulled back from her face and shoulders. The lesson starts with barre exercise. Diedra knows the five positions and a few of the exercises, but placement and turnout are not her forte. While counting for the class, the teacher quietly uses her own toe to correct Diedra's feet. Floor combinations follow barre; choreography is last. When the ninety-minute lesson ends, Diedra is told that she should attend the preteen class, but that she will probably move up quickly once she has the basics down.

If we fast-forward through the next six years, we see Diedra taking one, two, then seven classes weekly including double jazz classes Monday and Wednesday evenings, double ballet class Saturday morning, followed by a hip-hop class at 1:00, after which Diedra grabs a quick lunch on her way back to the neighborhood studio where she started. There, she teaches two more hip-hop classes. Both studios and her room at home sport trophies from competitions in contemporary forms like hip-hop. She's spent three summers at conferences and camps, choreographed two musicals at her high school, and has been admitted into the professional dance company based at the Evanston studio. (Professional studios usually have their own dance company, which performs, competes and/or tours.)

Diedra has prepared audition tapes for applying to companies and colleges alike, including Julliard, Ballet West, and Oregon Ballet Theatre. She's applied for a scholarship to Northwestern University's famous theatre program, which would allow her to continue dancing in the professional Evanston company. All told, including daily stretches, she dances more than 20 hours per week, maintains a 3.0 GPA at school to support her college applications, and attends professional performances or reviews videos on an average of another hour weekly. Her training program is her own, built from her ambition, the support of her mother, and the recommendations of professionals and peers. Nor is she unique. Her serious peers—about 20 of the 50 to 60 people who show up for class regularly—all follow similar schedules. Professional publications support and inform her with articles on dance careers. Her teachers continue to make recommendations regarding classes and studios that will extend and strengthen her abilities.

During Diedra's junior year, Emily, a girl from Texas whom Diedra met at a summer conference, comes to board with Diedra and her mom and enrolls at Diedra's high school for her senior year so that she can study jazz at the Evanston studio and ballet at a studio in Chicago. When she turns eighteen, Emily signs up with a modeling agency in the City and her occasional catalog work and jeans ads pay for her mother to fly up from Texas for visits. Emily's goal is the New York City Ballet, or at least dance work on or off Broadway. As soon as she graduates, she will supplement her dance classes schedule with acting and voice lessons, paid for by modeling work. She will move to New York the following year, when Diedra will graduate and move to LA.

Diedra's goal is to join a ballet company (with income approximately equal to a public school teacher). If she is very lucky, she will get work in television commercials, on a weekly show, or in a film, where she will make much more money for a shorter time. Whatever level she reaches will depend not only on the quality of her work, but also a great deal on the teachers with whom she chooses to study and the networking opportunities they are able to bring her. The stage will consider her movement, presence and figure; television and film will be concerned with her face, as well, and probably her voice and acting ability. She will need to find the best coaches in each area. She will find the highest quality of instruction, the highest level of peer work (to learn from), and the best network of connections studying with coaches who have the strongest national reputations. Position and reputation come from the achievements of coaches and their students, i.e., from how *well*, not how *long* they've worked.

Financially, she may apply for a scholarship to colleges or may audition to study with a ballet company. (The corps de ballet is paid, though often not much.) Teachers often give carte blanche to students who take more than three or four classes weekly, allowing the student to pay one fee for unlimited classes. Teaching a weekly class already gets Diedra a free pass for her own lessons. All gear and dancewear is the student's responsibility; the studio may sell some shoes or dancewear, particularly with the studio's logo.

Wherever Diedra's work, ambition, and talent take her, she will teach. Whether she teaches to pay for her lessons, subs for the master teacher, choreographs for a company, or decides to open a studio, it's an unwritten law: you pay back. She will draw students based on her reputation as a dancer as well as her skill as a teacher, even as a sub. For example, if Diedra, as an advanced student and member of the professional dance company, is considered by fellow students as less than thorough in teaching warmups and choreography, classes will be lightly attended the days she subs for the master teacher—something she wants to avoid. She is already building her reputation by her ability to take class (learn), apply it (perform), and give it back (teach).

Not all dance students want to become professional; most dance simply for the joy and the exercise. Yet *the same assessments are used for all students in every dance studio in the world.* First position is always the same, within the same form. Second is second. Fifth is fifth. (In French and Russian forms of ballet, positions differ slightly; jazz form is parallel rather than turned out.) Turnout is turnout; extension is extension; pullup is pullup. And, by the same set of standards, late is late (as in counting), and sloppy is sloppy. The degree to which these universal standards are exacted in each studio and from each dancer determines the reputation of that studio or dancer and, hence, placement on the professional spiral. Whether one's dance education is a week long or lifelong, the standards are set by the best performers, past and present, and disseminated globally.

Disseminated how? Companies tour; some give master classes on tour. Film, television and video have vastly expanded the dancer's network, as have journals such as *Dance Magazine,* and regional, national, and international organizations, conferences, workshops and competitions. Dancers observe, learn, incorporate. Ballet is over six hundred years old. Modern dance was assimilated into the professional performance and studio dance system around 1900, first in Germany, later in Russia and later still in the United States; jazz dance followed in the 1930s in America and spread to other countries. Breakdancing, hip-hop, and other forms of street dancing joined the studio system in the '80s. Gymnastics and figure skating both have dance components, for which Olympians spend at least some time studying in the dance studio system or with a studio-trained coach or choreographer.

In the United States, there is no flowchart of governing bodies, no teacher certification, or written standardized testing. Teachers/coaches, studios, techniques, styles, forms, and students come and go, as in a living ecosystem. Advancement is based on one's own work and that of one's company and/or students. Acting, art, figure skating, gymnastics, martial arts, piano, skiing, swimming, tennis, and voice students all participate in separate but similar systems. These systems grow, expand, change, include, assimilate, and evolve—living, open systems—while continuing to produce the majority of the finest artists and athletes in the world, year after year.

Or not.

Not producing means not eating. Parents and students vote with their feet. Most beginning teacher-coaches in these fields are paid far less than public school teachers, and they're paid not at all for students who aren't there. Coaches who do not or cannot produce results for their students simply find other work or teach just for fun. Those who produce favorable results do something impossible in the public school system: They advance. They earn the right to move up because there is a place to go. With advancement come more students, more prestigious venues, and, at the very top, more money, better projects, and the very best students.

Conversely, students seek out the best teachers regionally, those who have studied with the best teachers nationally, who have studied with the best teachers internationally, creating a web or network. For example, I knew growing up that my piano teacher had studied with a teacher at Oberlin College, who had studied with Nadia Boulanger in New York, who had studied with a teacher in Europe, who had studied with Beethoven.

When I opened my performing arts school in 1975, I did everything: I scheduled classes, designed advertising copy, found space to rent, found other teachers to rent space from me in return for inclusion in my marketing. I designed course offerings, enrolled students, joined the local chamber of commerce, joined professional organizations in music, theatre and dance and attended their conferences. I maintained my certification to teach various methods, increased my own training, founded a children's performing company where students could use what they learned, vacuumed the floor, cleaned the toilet, paid the insurance and utilities, and taught. I had about four years' teaching experience, had run two music schools, and had done the master schedule for a performing arts summer program in Paris. Yet in the beginning there were times I quite literally didn't eat.

Then my reputation grew sufficiently and my performing company became popular enough that we became the resident company at a city-owned theatre facility where I could direct full-time. Eventually my company toured throughout the state, and I wrote, designed, directed and produced three original musicals, one under the tutelage of Anthony Newley. I made about as much money as a first-year public school elementary teacher, minus benefits. But, I experienced autonomy and creativity, student and personal growth, achievement, fulfillment, and acclaim that I have seldom witnessed in public schools outside those rare exceptions like Jaime Escalante and Mavis Collins. It was a tremendous amount of work—as all teaching is—but with an enormous personal payoff for my students, for me.

While coaches' reputations, choice of jobs and, sometimes, compensation are all based on what they are able to do, they have the autonomy to do what needs to be done. If one idea, method, or set of materials isn't working for them, they can chuck it and try a new one. They don't have to close their doors, wait for approval (bureaucratic sanction) or beg forgiveness (default approval). They are bound to other teachers through professional organizations which often provide training, standards and criteria for judging results. Membership is voluntary or earned, except for unionized professional performers, where membership is compulsory. From coaches for the Special Olympics to Broadway choreographers, from summer theatre directors to city recreation program teachers, reputations rise and fall on personal knowledge and ability and student achievement. Again, parents and students vote with their feet.

Swimming offers a parallel athletic example. Youngsters are grouped primarily by ability, secondarily by age. For example, a twelve-year-old nonswimmer will be placed with other nonswimmers, regardless of age, not with other twelve-year-olds who are learning to dive. Those showing talent or wanting to compete will gravitate to and be guided toward swim schools, swim teams or coaches who can accommodate them. Those with special needs will seek out the programs and coaches who can accommodate them.

Exceptional talents will follow a schedule similar to Diedra's. Without going into equal detail, it should be easy to see the parallels between the athletic coaching model and the arts studio model. Athletes belong to teams, clubs, associations, and international organizations in much the same network design as artists, though many sports are far more structured. Again, the best athletes set the standards for the world and those standards are disseminated throughout the network right out to the backyard swim schools, the neighborhood Tae Kwon Do schools, and the local Little Leagues.

In both the arts and athletics, teachers/coaches are predisposed to look for, foster and promote talent. Focusing on the positive keeps open systems healthy. Public schools are predisposed to look for and eliminate problems. Problems disturb equilibrium. We spend as much as five times more on special education students as on gifted students. We provide tutoring and intervention services for at-risk students. From the public school perspective it seems almost ludicrous to think that gifted students need extra services. We'll return to this point in Chapter 6.

Figure 4–1
Open System Spiral Organization Chart

Academic Models

Before we examine two nonpublic academic systems with open designs, it's important to emphasize that what we are looking at is the *design of the system*, not the pedagogical method or even the school itself. The purpose here is to look at how schools are associated, at the position of the teacher within the school and system, at the way the system is unified, and at the ability of the system to grow, change, and evolve.

Waldorf Schools

Waldorf schools are found throughout the world, from Honolulu to Detroit, South Africa to Nepal. National and local branches of the Waldorf Schools' Association advise and counsel startups and existing schools, helping to insure that Rudolf Steiner's pedagogical philosophy is understood and followed. The Association of Waldorf Schools of North America (AWSNA) was begun in 1965, thirty-seven years after the first North American school was founded in New York City.

Formed as a vehicle for sharing experience and support among schools, AWSNA now includes a publishing arm, a bookstore, and a website. Waldorf schools are independent, self-governed and self-responsible. To start a Waldorf school, one needs to declare the intent to the Association and in turn will receive information and support with Waldorf curriculum, descriptions of common Waldorf practices and suggestions. Individuals also belong to the association.

AWSNA and the many other Waldorf associations worldwide act as a cooperative, providing services and materials as needed by their member schools. Individual schools vary with their founders and communities but carry the common thread of

Steiner's philosophy and the common goal of making school a positive experience for all students. The schools themselves and the associations are free to evolve, grow, implement change, open, close, join forces, institute new programs. Direction comes from the teachers, based on the needs of students and their parents. Individual schools or subgroups are free to range from unconventional to dogmatic without getting a waiver (like public schools) to do so.

Montessori Schools

> *Montessori* means different things to different people and sometimes different things to the same person. Montessorians themselves may disagree on what constitutes the core of Montessori education and philosophy. (Gordon, in Shapiro and Hellen 1998, 5)

The system founded by Maria Montessori in Italy has two associations in the United States, the Association Montessori Internationale (AMI) and the American Montessori Society (AMS). AMI was founded by Dr. Montessori herself and is run by her granddaughter, Rinilde. It is a United Nations Non-Governmental Organization whose purpose is to train and certificate teachers and accredit schools. All AMI schools must hire only AMI-trained teachers.

Each school, regardless of which association it belongs to, is largely autonomous. There are proprietary schools, run by an owner-founder, as well as nonprofit schools and some public schools. There are preschools, elementary, middle and high schools. While "there is no single body that accredits Montessori schools" (Shapiro and Hellen 1998, 4), there are, according to Mary Maher Boehnlein who pioneered the Reading Recovery

programs used in public education, six criteria of an authentic Montessori school (Shapiro and Hellen 1998, 9). They include teacher training, classroom equipment, child groupings, school days, classroom aide, and curriculum.

> Montessori education has developed in a variety of ways in North America. Some schools adhere quite closely to the initial specifications, others have adapted freely.... But it is important to recognize that although classrooms that take the name *Montessori* may look somewhat different, they all may be quite successful in meeting children's needs and nourishing their potential. (Shapiro and Hellen 1998, 11)

For all schools, whether "authentic" or not, there are definite guidelines as to teacher-student ratio, curriculum, age groupings, and the number and training of teachers. The Montessori Accreditation Council for Teacher Education (MACTE), founded in 1991, is widely used for teacher training.

Montessori is a perfect example of a living system: one that gave birth to a second system with its own new ideas and outlook; one that coexists and thrives alongside its own offspring. Individual schools, too, can evolve. This is a system based around the teacher and students, founded on a pedagogical philosophy that addresses human learning, and flexible enough to allow adaptation, growth, change and evolution. Association is for mutual benefit, not top-down compliance. Teachers are not at the bottom of a bureaucratic dog pile but at the center of a supporting web.

Arguments

Readers who didn't quite make it out of The Box at the inception of this chapter are no doubt furious by now (if, indeed, they're still reading). "But only a few people learn to dance or are even inter-

ested. *Everyone* has to learn math, has to learn to read!" True. It's equally true that only a minority of students take French or jewelry making or calculus—or are even interested—but public schools teach these subjects, so universality is moot.

Another favorite argument against other academic systems is that they cater to the well-off and to students whose parents get involved. This is akin to arguing that we shouldn't aim CDs at youngsters or release children's movies because the parents of poor children cannot afford them or may not want to or know how to get involved with them. Of course the parents of at-risk students buy them CDs, let them go to movies, and watch TV with them.

The point is, *people get involved in what's important to them.* As any member of a School Attendance Review Board (SARB) can attest, despite compulsory attendance laws, school is simply not important to many people. *At-risk* is our term, not theirs, because they are not playing our game according to our rules. Once again, parents and students vote with their feet, but we, in our 19th-century legislated monopoly just haven't been paying attention. We might be surprised by what happened if we did.

This brings us to the objection that public education is compulsory, regardless of interest, motivation, (dis)advantage or (dis)ability: another structure firmly ensconced inside The Box. While there are ways other than compulsory attendance to insure an educated populace, and plenty of evidence to show that far from "everybody" is currently being educated anyway, compulsory education is another book.

For purposes of this book, let's assume that academic education will remain compulsory. In that case, our protest relates more directly to the idea that some kids are very difficult to teach in our public system: They have severe disadvantages or special needs, are unable to speak, read or write English at grade level, or are highly

unmotivated. American students are the most diverse population on earth. Public schools have an immensely challenging task trying to teach all these students to read, write, calculate, understand the democratic process and the scientific method, and relate history to current events. That's obvious and it's all the more reason to develop alternatives rather than insist on one-size-fits-all.

Standing outside The Box, it's obvious that the inherent difficulties in educating our diverse students are exponentially exacerbated when placed within a system built around conformity and standardization!

Doors: Potential Escape Routes

Catherine Ponder said, "It's amazing how fast doors open to us when we dare to take control of a situation" (Zadra and Carlson 1995). Before concluding, it's appropriate to note those "doors" out of The Box that are currently available to us. So-called "magnet" schools have been around long enough that many of them have seen the pendulum reverse and have been reconverted back into neighborhood schools. The point of magnets or "schools of choice" is voluntary integration and the state-administered federal dollars that follow—so-called "Voluntary Integration Program" (VIP) funds. Magnets have allowed schools to focus on particular themes or approaches to instruction, like performing arts, science and technology, parent participation, back-to-basics, community-as-campus, etc. Magnets are a small step away from the bureaucracy, a first step toward an alternative system.

Charter schools operate in many states now, usually under laws far less restrictive than regular public schools. Charters come in a variety of configurations and often belong to charter schools associations, much like the open systems schools we explored earlier in Chapter 4. We must beware, because these schools are still under the direct control of the current public system and legislators are fond of chipping away at their freedoms until they begin to look like regular public schools. Nevertheless, charters operate with more freedom than other public schools.

This freedom usually takes the form of fewer restrictions on where money may be spent, modifications to curriculum content (provided standards are met), choice in texts, school themes or specializations such as technology, the ability to hire nonunion personnel, to hire noncredentialed experts or consulting teachers, and to do away with tenure. Like magnets, many charters have a particular schoolwide focus, like the arts, a particular reading program, parent and/or community involvement, or a particular philosophy. For example, there are Montessori charter schools, charters on wheels (traveling schools) and charters online. Because charters have their own associations, their greatest ties with public education are funding and standards. They represent the only current public alternative system and they need to be strengthened, not subjugated, if public education is to survive in any viable form.

Vouchers continue to be a topic of hot debate. Teachers' unions are convinced they'll ruin public education. This is an overreaction, to say the least. First, vouchers could be controlled by both state and local statutes to insure school populations demographically consistent with their locale. Second, anyone who has ever done so can tell you that starting a school is no easy task nor is keeping one open. Once started, there is no guarantee of survival. The idea that, with vouchers, hundreds of "storefront schools" would open, that unqualified and unscrupulous people would try to get rich off unsuspecting students is simply ludicrous. Nobody's going to get rich off a publicly funded school (unless they're textbook publishers) but they could easily get worn out.

Moreover, in the new environment created by the standards and accountability craze, no voucher-funded school is going to stay open unless it's producing results. (Only public schools do that.) At-risk students will *not* be excluded because, unlike in private education, they each represent just as much income as any other student. In fact, they usually carry more dollars in the way of federal and state "categorical" funding aimed at leveling the playing field. And, it can be easier to show growth in test scores with students at the bottom of the range than with students at the top. Vouchers have the potential to be the beginning of an alternative system of customized schools regulated by agreed-upon standards of excellence.

While these doors exist in the public system, we owe it to students and to ourselves to explore the positive possibilities related to them. We must not hide in terror behind illogical fears that they'll ruin everything or unfounded claims that they'll exclude people. We're already doing a fine job of both. Instead of getting irate over the negative things we think they could do, perhaps we should get creative over the positive things they might do.

Plato said, "We can easily forgive a child who is afraid of the dark; the real tragedy of life is when men are afraid of the light" (Schiller 1999).

5

Enter: Theseus

*To see, one must go beyond the imagination and for that
one must stand absolutely still as though at the center of
a leap.*

—JOHN CAGE (Schiller 1999)

Procrustes was a mean old man whose acquaintance one makes when studying Latin or Greek mythology. His enormous house stood by a lonely road in the mythological Attican countryside. Travelers caught by nightfall and seeking shelter found that Procrustes had but one guest bed, and one grave idiosyncrasy: His guests must fit that bed. Thus he measured everyone, tying all to the iron bedstead and stretching those too short, dismembering those too tall. Theseus slew Procrustes and we must do it again.

After World War II, W. Edwards Deming tried to convince American business that its 19th-century hierarchical bureaucratic structure was outmoded, costly, inefficient and in need of replacing. U.S. corporations wouldn't listen, so he went to Japan. Japanese business listened and in record time turned a conquered economy with inferior quality products into a force that threatened our economy. *Then* we listened and the rest is history. We have much to take credit for in the efforts we have all put into education. But, we will have a lot to answer for if we continue to ignore the structure that is definitely holding us back.

This is crucial: Once we grasp that we need a more flexible and diverse structure, we must *let go.*

We must rid ourselves of the idea that one system, one structure, one adopted method, adopted textbook, one standardized test can provide the best possible education for all students. We are too diverse in too many areas—ethnicity, language, age, learning styles, interests, talents, and special needs, to name but a few. *We must face the fact that use of a single system does not in any way assure either quality or equity.* We must realize that our system is structured for uniformity and will continually try to bring diversity back to "center," back to the one size that definitely does not fit all. We must stop spoon-feeding curriculum just because it's in the text, regardless of whether students already know it or whether it holds any relevance for them. As Castaneda said, "Power rests on the kind of knowledge one holds. What is the sense of knowing things that are useless?" (1968, 24). Education needs to be a *means* to growth, not an end in itself. Are we capable of grasping this?

One Saturday morning at a required all-day class, there were two teachers doing a talking heads routine for new administrators. True to form, they never bothered to ask whether some of us already knew any of the material they were going to spend six hours talking about. They had their agenda; if it bored us to death, that was irrelevant. The feeling seemed to be that because there were two of them and they took turns, and because they instructed us to do group activities (into which we had no input), the class would be interesting and useful. The Two-Talking-Heads-Are-Better-Than-One theory.

At the first break, I ran out to my car, cranked up a Stevie Ray Vaughn CD, slid back the sunroof and zoomed out of there.

The class was so boring and such a waste of time I was almost ready to just leave and take my first-ever F. Instead, I went to Starbucks for a chai, where I saw some of my classmates. They complained they were getting nothing out of the class. I asked, "Then why don't we all just talk to the teachers?" They didn't want to. I probed, "Why not? How are they going to improve the class if we don't tell them?"

Their answer?

Are you ready?

This is really good.

Remember: These are educators in charge of teachers and instruction at their school sites.

Sitting down?

Here's their reason:

They didn't really see how else it could be taught.

Goody. No wonder we throw so many pigs off the roof! We have no clue what else to do.

The point is that here was a graduate level class for the very people who lead and evaluate teachers, curriculum and instruction, and it was being taught in the same one-size model we see in classrooms all the way to kindergarten. If you can stand one more irony, the class topic was handling "change" in education!

Projects that are

- personally relevant
- hands-on
- real-world-based
- immediately applicable
- embedded with concepts transferable across the curriculum and into one's life
- differentiated to be individually challenging and modally diverse

have been recommended by experts from John Dewey in the 30s to Linda Darling-Hammond and Howard Gardner in the 90s. But, try as we might, this type of teaching continually eludes us in our present system.

Those of us "mavericks" who actually teach using such projects may be looked upon with skepticism by other teachers and administrators alike. We're literally not on the same page as was agreed upon weekly during our grade-level meetings. Administrators may find the level of kinesthetic student activity in our classrooms as disturbing as our lack of traditional work stapled to the walls. (Where in the real world do we find stuff stapled to walls?)

And our test scores? Well, when hands-on methods create higher scores, we probably cheated somehow or taught to the test. How could anything out of the norm *not* be suspect within the structure of our current one-way system? Notable educators who have done well with at-risk students—like Jaime Escalante (subject of the film *Stand and Deliver*)—have done so with very unconventional methods. They were sanctioned to use these methods within the current system only because everyone had given up on the kids with whom these teachers were working.

Teachers do not routinely practice these methods because they don't understand *how*, given the constraints of the system. Or they don't understand how *period*. Or they've never heard of them. Many, sadly, think they *are* practicing them! Other teachers have reacted to increased pressure for results, labels like "underperforming schools" and bombardment by research which may contradict earlier research. They begin to question their own skills, to doubt themselves. Thus, besides the system itself, there's obviously one more roadblock to reform: us.

We cover curriculum because that's what's *expected*, regardless of what reforms say. We sit in front of the class and *wah-wah-*

wah-wah-wah like the teacher in a Charlie Brown cartoon video by Charles Shultz. The quintessential talking head. We don't bother to find out what each student already knows or is interested in because that's not our job as the system defines (confines?) it. We expect students to behave, bring the required materials, and follow the book or handouts without disturbing others or disrupting our routine. Students receive the curriculum. Teachers deliver it.

Many, many teachers are aware—instinctively or explicitly—that something is amiss with our prescription. Why, then, aren't there more mavericks despite the system? Simple. The system doesn't breed them. In fact, it breeds the opposite.

The resistance we experience to change in our system is about much more than normal fear and discomfort. It's about us voluntarily and involuntarily supporting and *enabling* the system. It's about codependency. Codependency is the habitual behavior of helping, fixing, smoothing over, coping with, excusing and enabling others' dysfunctional behaviors. A wife making excuses for an alcoholic husband. Employees making excuses for the system where they work.

Anne Wilson Schaef and Diane Fassel detail why we react in these ways in their work, *The Addictive Organization* (1988). They list and describe characteristics of addiction including:

- confusion
- perfectionism
- a belief in scarcity
- crisis orientation
- depression
- stress
- negativism
- defensiveness
- tunnel vision
- fear

In Chapter 4 I alluded to the fact that many public educators feel any programs, theories, designs or even results from outside public education are invalid inside the public system. In effect, they are correct. The system doesn't allow for outside input and will simply assimilate or invalidate it in order to return to equilibrium.

> Invalidation is the process the addictive system uses to define into nonexistence those ideas and experiences that the system cannot know, understand, or most importantly, control. Invalidation is one of the main hallmarks of a closed system. It acknowledges that divergent ideas exist but will not let them into the frame of reference of the system *and* it refuses even to recognize the existence of processes that are threatening to it. (Schaef and Fassel 1988, 70)

We take it personally when a student is moved out of our class to another, when a parent doesn't like the way we teach. "In an addictive system, we tend to judge our success by how other people perceive us" (Schaef and Fassel 1988).

We attempt to pick up everyone else's slack and make unworkable situations seem workable. The city doesn't have a transit system? Fine. The school district will provide buses! (Then we'll let those buses, rather than pedagogical reasons, dictate our school schedule.) Parents can't afford to pay for food for all their children? Do we ask the community where they live to find them jobs? Do we educate parents to consider having only as many children as they can feed and educate? No! We provide a federal program to let the kids eat at school. Not enough money for paper for the classrooms during the last two months of school? No problem! Teachers will buy it out of their own pockets.

The list is long and completely taken for granted. We cover for, put up with, take on responsibilities ourselves rather than place the ownership where it belongs. We "fix things," blame the wrong people (ourselves, or other casualties of the system). We cling firmly, desperately, blindly to the idea that things are "getting better" or are "not so bad." If we could open our eyes to them, we would begin to recognize such prevalent behaviors for what they are. We could form a national Educators' Al-Anon with local chapters. Then, maybe we could move on!

To design parallel, open educational systems suitable in the new millennium, we need people willing to let go of the teacher's manual, the recipes, the publishers' scripts. We need people willing to begin to use their minds and hearts fully and in new ways (see Dr. Martin Krovetz' definition of resiliency in his book, *Fostering Resiliency*). That's what we say we'd like our kids to do. Shouldn't we go first? We need to understand our system's design. We need to look realistically at the world we live in and change our current thinking to fit our world and to insure a future. We need to make a leap of faith. We need to risk so our students will not remain at-risk.

We will make mistakes. Let's face it: We make them every day already. We're human. We must treat our mistakes as opportunities for learning, not as failures. The only mistake we cannot afford to make (because we cannot learn from it) is to cling steadfastly to the old and refuse to budge.

The first time I went snorkeling in Hawaii I was excited, eager. I need to mention that I am a true Capricorn, earth sign, mountain climbing, landlubber goat, not much of a swimmer. But, I had a life vest and fins and I was raring to go. 'Til it was time to let go of the boat. Looking down through thirty feet of water, I decided that stuff was way too transparent to be trusted beneath my little hooves. I'd just hang onto the boat, thank you very much.

Try as they might, they could not convince me to let go. Not until someone gave me a "Boogie board." I was ecstatic! Now here was something to hold onto. You could hang on it, lie on it, wrap yourself around it. Okay! Now we're talking. I might have been the last one off the boat, but I was also the last one back on. I had a great time. All the turtles swam with me. They must have figured any human with both a life vest and a Boogie board was no big threat. I figured snorkeling was just about the most fun one could have in a day. So long as I had something to hang onto, I didn't need the boat.

Pick your Boogie board: an open system with which you are familiar, a thematic approach that works well for you, a type of student you feel best equipped to serve. And come on in. The water's fine.

6

The Parallel Systems Concept

If the future is to remain open and free, we need people who can tolerate the unknown, who will not need the support of completely worked-out systems or traditional blueprints from the past.
—MARGARET MEAD (Zadra and Carlson 1995)

We cannot change the design of our current system. That would require dismantling the system, which would be ludicrous, unnecessary, and probably impossible, anyway. Instead, we should focus our energies on allowing, developing and nurturing new, parallel, alternative systems that will function alongside the old.

Consider alternative medicine as an example. A decade ago, *Time Magazine* ran a cover story on the alternative medicine industry, citing it as grossing $27 billion annually, at that time serving about 30% of Americans, and growing rapidly due to a general dissatisfaction with conventional medicine. Listing several of Western medicine's best achievements, the article also pointed out what it termed "serious weak spots" like its impersonal, one-size-fits-all approach (Wallis 1991, 68). Conventional medicine is a hierarchical bureaucracy, like our education system and the post office—all closed, mechanical systems designs. Indeed, the bureaucracy and red tape relating to health care have taken it out of the reach of millions of Americans without the requisite insurance.

The U.S. Postal Service (USPS), too, earned enormous criticism from the public for its slowness and inefficiency and the inescapable long lines at local offices. The USPS, like American business after Japanese business cut into our market share, has made some organizational changes. Not by choice. The Internet, email, voicemail, faxes and cell phones, plus Federal Express and UPS (both companies that redesigned using Deming-style methods) have made it possible for about one-third of us to simply not use the post office very much at all. It's become a conveyor of holiday cards and our largest source of junk mail, which we tend to open right next to the recycling bin, trash bin or shredder.

Conventional medicine, on the other hand, has yet to reorganize its monolithic structure and continues to receive battering by press, politicians, and the public. Meanwhile, more people turn to alternative medicine because it works as well or better than conventional medicine for chronic conditions and is often more easily available and more personal. From chiropractic to yoga, from tai chi to acupuncture, from massage therapy to herbal supplements, people find greater *wellness* than with traditional practice. Herein lies an important concept.

So-called "Eastern" and indigenous practices, upon which alternative therapies are based, concentrate on *health*, not disease. What makes people well? At ease? What has happened to that something when they "fall ill"? How can they be brought back from dis-ease to ease? This views the person as a whole, noting all the life factors that contribute to dis-ease and working with the patient to maintain a proper, balanced lifestyle. It's a preventative viewpoint whose standard is *perfection*—how everything operates when the patient is functioning at highest potential. It is said that in ancient China, doctors were paid for people to stay healthy.

When one fell ill, the doctor had failed and had to bring the patient back to wellness at his own expense!

Conventional Western medicine is, of course, focused on health, but the approach is through the study of disease, not of wellness. In their training, doctors dissect corpses (where, obviously, wellness has failed) and make rounds of hospital patients to study their diseases. I mention this simply because in education we, too, study failure. Why can't some students read? What constitutes academic disability? How do we help "troubled" readers, "at-risk" students, anyone whose learning needs or styles don't fit our Procrustean approach? Rarely do we study our "gifted" students. In fact, we may ignore them. ("They'll do fine on their own.") Often we have no clue *what* to do with them. At times we even seem embarrassed by them.

Worse yet, we do it intentionally. At an educators' international conference in San Francisco, I attended a workshop on multiple intelligences and gifted students. The presenter started with a brief seven-question quiz covering all "official" intelligence areas. The questions were extremely basic for anyone with a rudimentary background in each area (music, for instance). All could be answered with knowledge gained in public schools. Because the test was simple for me, I assumed it would be simple for many of the 200 other educators in the room as well.

I assumed wrong. After we went over the answers, the presenter asked all those scoring 100% to stand. Again, I assumed there would be lots of us. Wrong, again. I was alone. And, that roomful of fellow educators who had chosen to attend a seminar on working with the gifted? They booed my 100%. Good-natured booing? Some of it, yes. But, I've come to understand in my years in public education that educators from the classroom to the district office (D.O.) often make disparaging comments about gifted students and don't really like them very much.

At a D.O. meeting, I added "gifted" students to a brain-storming list of types of diversity found in the classroom and I thought my fellow administrators would eat me alive. Gifted kids don't fit into the covered curriculum. They often have parents who are vocal. They make extra work and we don't quite know what to do with them so we give them twenty problems when we give the rest of the class ten. Besides, why *should* we worry about them? They're smart. They'll get by. No problem.

Often, there is an immediate problem. These are the kids who are so bored they become disruptive. Kids like this (often boys) are simply labeled "troublemakers" and are never even recognized as gifted. A second grader was passed on to me one year and I was told to watch out for him: He had no "social conscience" or feelings, and he made other kids cry for no reason. Of course I watched him. Quickly I discovered that, having a very agile brain and a great deal of prior knowledge, he had been bored to death. I began giving him more difficult work, putting him in charge of things, giving him problems to solve at his level. He bloomed. This "antisocial" kid became very nurturing to other kids as he whizzed through both the second and third grade curriculum that year. Interest, self-direction, happiness and observable growth are great motivators.

In our alternative artistic and athletic models, a good coach treats all fairly and with respect, but reserves one-on-one time for those with the most potential and some extra time for those with the most problems. Students in over their heads and those too advanced will be directed to a more suitable class. That's assuming they somehow made it past the pre-assessment and got into the wrong class in the first place!

Our structure locks us into particular classes and grades without sufficient regard to student readiness. The result? A typical California district's budget shows 500% to 600% more money for students needing extra help than for gifted students. Where could these students be—where could our future be—if we truly challenged them? A Silicon Valley engineer told me in the fall of 2000, his research facility had 1500 openings they could not find college graduates qualified to fill. But then, they weren't looking for "at risk" employees. If we offer alternative education focused on the positive, no doubt everyone's achievement could rise and jobs like these could be filled with workers educated in America.

During the summer of 1999, I served as Principal for a remedial middle school summer school program. We pre-assessed all students and made it a requirement that they achieve an A+ on their post-assessment. Most of these "at risk" students had rarely gotten an A on anything, let alone an A+, but the goal was set. Teachers and students focused on perfection, rather than passing. At the end of six weeks, 98% of them made it. The other 2% all achieved a C or above. Between the pre- and postassessments, the student body overall showed 147% growth in test scores in six weeks.

Did anyone from the district ever ask how we accomplished this? No, of course not. Do they realize that 147% growth is like buying gasoline for $1 per gallon on June 15th and $2.47 per gallon on July 31st? Probably not. No attempt will be made to replicate this alternative approach in our public system. Alternative schools using a variety of approaches like this one could succeed with many students who do not currently find success in our traditional system.

Now let's define our living systems model.

7

Defining Open Systems

*You can have the results you say you want, or you can
have all the reasons why you can't have them. But you
can't have both. Reasons or results. You get to choose.*
        —SUSAN CARLSON (Zadra and Carlson 1995)

A ccording to Capra, three interdependent criteria describe
living systems: pattern, structure, and process. Basing his
synthesis on the work of Maturana, Varela, Prigogine, and
Bateson, he goes on to define each of these:

> *pattern of organization:* the configuration of rela-
> tionships that determines the system's essential
> characteristics
>
> *structure:* the physical embodiment of the system's
> pattern of organization
>
> *life process:* the activity involved in the continual
> embodiment of the system's pattern of organization
> (1996, 160)

In living systems the pattern of organization is characterized by
autopoesis — by self-creation. Process is identified with cognition.
Living systems grow, change and evolve within their basic pattern

of organization. What would a school system look like based on this model?

The Open School System

Open, "living" systems—by the very changes they encourage—have a way of blending into the landscape of life. In many cases, as we have seen in the dance studio example in Chapter 4, they do not appear to be systems at all because of the autonomy retained by structures which are networked together and supported by a common set of standards.

Teachers within these systems associate freely with other teachers. There are regular opportunities (performances, meets) where both students and coaches get immediate, relevant feedback on how they're doing. While the achievements of "superstars" constantly serve to raise the bar and set a standard, coaches strive to produce results across their team and throughout their schools. If we used living superstars in math, logic, science, writing, public speaking, and social science as examples, the standards movement would make more sense to everyone, especially students. Some elementary teachers will read to students about a particular author's life. A few will even get that author to come speak at their school. It's these examples that establish real, living standards toward which kids are self-motivated to work. Alternative systems could be free to focus more on this type of standard and less on the more seemingly arbitrary, "What am I ever gonna use this stuff for?" ones established by education departments and textbook publishers.

Alternative programs do not operate in equilibrium. They do not stay one size, but evolve and grow, give birth to new programs, get outmoded and replaced, as we saw with the Montessori system. Teachers have a high degree of autonomy without constraint of specific strategies, texts and "coverage." Results must speak for themselves. Local, national and international associations provide training, guidelines, accreditations, materials, competitions, conferences, master classes, grants or scholarships, and more. The teacher is the focus, the center of a hub or web or the nucleus of a living system, linked to other teachers, to supports and to guidelines as in a web. Information flows back and forth, impelling growth, change and evolution.

> The emerging next step in distributed intelligence is self-organizing systems of all kinds. Hierarchical control systems have one centralized boss, human or computerized, telling everyone what to do and enforcing commands through layers of authority. Distributed intelligence, in contrast, uses many decentralized decision makers of comparable power, interpreting events under shared rules, interacting with and learning from each other, and controlling their collective behavior through the interaction of their diverse local decisions, much like an ecosystem works. (Hawken, Lovins, and Lovins 1999, 67)

Because they operate far from equilibrium, open systems "best able to coordinate complex and flexible behavior, best able to adapt and evolve" operate at the "edge of chaos" (Capra 1996, 204). The word *chaos* in this sense is specific to science and mathematics and has little to do with our colloquial use of it or with words like *chaotic*. The mathematics that support chaos theory were developed in the 20th century, furthered by the use of computers for high-speed repetitive calculations. Like the mathematics supporting the study of living systems and developments in microprocessors, they stretch the laws of mechanical Newtonian physics in order to accurately describe the behavior of living systems.

Most of us have seen computer-generated drawings called *fractals*. Usually pictures of ferns or intricate geometric shapes, they are plotted using fractal geometry developed by Benoit

Mandelbrot and they help illustrate a relatively new concept in science that randomness tends toward order (Land and Jarman 1992, 107). Open systems may *appear* to have little structure because that structure is both flexible and evolving; it provides a frame and pulls the system forward. In alternative educational systems order is present, focused around the teacher/coach as center and regulated by the growth results that teachers produce in all students as well as in themselves. The seeming randomness of separate programs becomes order when viewed from the bigger, systemic picture.

Coming from such a system, I found that in public schools I often felt like I was working with both hands tied behind my back. In my work as an administrator that feeling has increased. Many other public educators feel similar constraints. Without benefit of having worked in a system lacking such constraints, they have little confidence that it is possible or desirable to remove them.

Let's try.

A School Prototype

Let's look at some school concept prototypes for an alternative system. First we need teachers. (You can have hundreds of students, but without a teacher, you have no school [Black 1997, 18].) Let's say we have two teachers, one with visual arts, the other with performing arts training and certification. We now have potential projects to shape our school structure. One project will be musical theatre production; a second will be community murals. These teachers' expertise is with middle school students, so enrollment will begin there with students interested in the visual and performing arts.

The musical theatre production project will include all creative, technical, and performance areas. In math, review of all basic pre-algebra skills will be woven into set and costume building and choreography. Algebra will be integrated into set, lighting and costume design. Reading and writing can obviously be tied to script, as can history. Human health and biology can be introduced through dance and singing, physical science through stage management's operation of scenery and through lighting (Black 1997, 58–64). Books, texts and expert coaches will supplement project requirements so students can pass ongoing assessments and annual standardized tests in each subject area.

How do we know whether our students' achievement is on target? We assess them: before, during and after instruction. We adopt high standards from the beginning—at least as high, if not higher, than those being set by states across the country. We continually adjust curriculum and methods to suit our students and support their reaching the standards. The pattern of organization is the arts coaching model. The structure is the project. Standards and ongoing assessment create the life process.

Another school, School B, might be on a bus. That's the pattern of organization, a mobile school. Students will go on day trips, sometimes returning to the same spot for a week or two, and occasionally on week-long excursions. Curriculum will be standard school fare delivered in the traditional manner as well as through the "continuous field trip" approach and will determine the destinations. That's the structure. Standards and assessment again regulate the open, "life process," as with all example schools.

School C's pattern of organization is running a business. K–8 students will design, produce and sell goods at the school, from a storefront, or over the Web. Structure will depend on the teachers. All elements of running a business—from financial planning to writing promotional copy, from environmental impact reports to historical research—will frame curriculum and add structure.

School D is a feeder high school on the business campus of a chip manufacturer (pattern of organization) where the project takes the shape of apprenticeships (structure). School E focuses on traditional basic academics (pattern) where the project is providing homework support—an "Ask Us How" Web page—on the Internet. Guest lecturers may give workshops in their professional fields from physics and engineering to cooking both to round out curriculum and provide advanced level study. (Both: process.)

Again, in each school, all students will be assessed in all subject areas before the year begins, during the year, and at year end, with growth charted and compared to internal school goals and to other schools across the state, nation, globe. Curriculum and teachers can change, grow, and evolve based on assessment results as well as any number of other factors. Assessments maintain a constant accountability structure and projects-based instruction remains the open system's pattern of organization. The life process of the school is thematic. The theme addresses the interests and aptitudes of the teachers and students involved.

A Web of Schools

Since the schools themselves are providing the leadership, an association of these schools into something paralleling a district will provide support and group purchasing power for supplies and services. Like a cooperative, such a flexible alliance could continually readjust to serve the changing needs of the schools involved. In our living systems, our web of schools, teachers and students are at the center of the web, not the bottom of a dogpile.

It is possible to have schools where students want to be, choose to be. It is completely possible to group students by interest and skill level. To provide meaningful, relevant, real-world opportunities for *all* types of students to develop their interests and apply their knowledge and skills. To allow students to work to the full extent of their individual abilities and at their own best pace. To afford students opportunities to study with experts and masters in various fields. To better educate all students. Our previous arts, athletic and academic models (Chapter 4) are components to keep in mind when designing our overarching pattern of organization.

8

Open System Components

Invention is "a sudden cessation of stupidity."

Redesign requires "not so much having a new idea as stopping having an old idea."

—EDWIN LAND (Hawken, Lovins, and Lovins 1999, 64, 117)

In our arts, athletics and academic open system models, certain common threads or components emerge:

- student interest over coverage/conveyance
- standards and assessment
- customization
- focus on the top, the positive
- incentives and advancement
- apprenticeship: application and transference

Student Interest Over Coverage/Conveyance

First, student interest leads the way. The student wants certain knowledge and/or skills and pursues training. In public education, the student is *told* what knowledge and skills she *should* want and is expected to whip up some enthusiasm for learning them. On rare occasions, we'll find a teacher who actually asks students what they

Figure 8–1
Covering the Curriculum

want to learn. But, the overwhelming majority of teachers see their job as "covering curriculum"—curriculum mandated by people completely unfamiliar with individual teachers or students.

At an elementary school where I taught, I was grade level representative on a team of teachers who gave the principal input on issues pertaining to the staff and curriculum. One morning she asked about our math program—how we felt a particular publisher's series was working and whether it needed to be supplemented with another series.

One of the other teachers, a respected veteran of at least twenty years and our union representative, replied that she was hired by the district to teach the district curriculum, that the particular publisher's series was the adopted math program, and that, unless she was directed by the board to teach something else, that's what she'd teach. This is a fairly standard approach. This teacher is covering curriculum. She honestly believes that is her job.

Yeah? Well, if that's *not* her job, what *is*?

After she spoke, I turned to the principal and said, "I feel my job is to teach math, not a particular curriculum, and I'll use whatever resources I can find to make sure the kids learn it." Luckily, the principal was happy with my answer. Unfortunately, many would not be. Public school teachers, by and large, are still considered conveyors of information, sages on stages, talking heads. The national, state and federal bureaucrats decide what kids should know. Teachers "teach" this in the cubic zirconium version of teaching, that is, they convey the information.

Convey is not only accurate, it's systemic because a conveyor is integral to an assembly line, which, of course, is what we are. The bigwigs do the designing and make the decisions. The assembly line workers follow instructions, stamping out the same content over and over to the classes of kids who pass through their rooms. It is as though we all had the same needs and started with the same prior knowledge and learned at the same pace and same passive style and had the same interests and cared deeply about the subject matter. We don't. For a country priding itself on its "rugged individualists," we should have our heads examined for thinking we can turn out uniform products from our diverse population! Or should even want to!

While we convey or cover curriculum, student interest in what we're trying to cram down their throats will continue to have little importance in the average teacher's agenda, even though capturing it is the first step in student motivation. Our system is designed for conveyance, for moving people along—down prescribed paths at prescribed intervals, adding prescribed information in prescribed ways. We haven't quite agreed what to do when this doesn't work, because no one has the power to stop the assembly line.

Standards and Assessment

In an alternative system, how do we insure that all students still get where we want them to go? This question is almost as inevitable as it is illogical. First, we shouldn't be concerned with us all "still" getting there since we aren't all getting there now. Second, since creating different paths for different people better addresses our diversity, *more* people should get there. That's the whole point. Still, the question will be asked and, luckily, the answer is simple: assessment.

We already have standardized norm referenced tests available nationwide. While these are not the best assessment of student achievement, they are a start. The best assessments are "authentic"—that is, they test whether the student can actually apply and use the particular knowledge and skills being tested. California developed the California Assessment Program (CAP) in the early 1990s, replaced it with the California Learning Assessment System (CLAS) in the mid-1990s, and dropped both by the end of the decade. Although still paper-and-pencil tests, both were excellent steps in the direction of authentic assessment, but they were judged too costly to score and scores were deemed less reliable (in psychometric terms) than standardized tests.

Olympic scores are certainly not reliable in that sense, either, but we tend to accept them because the judges are experts in the field. The CLAS test scores were more reliable because scorers were given extensive training and scores had to agree in two to three readings of the same response. All papers were scored twice and any with major discrepancies were scored a third time. Reliability of scores and costs of scoring were cited when these tests were discontinued. The real problem was priorities.

True authentic assessments are easy to score. While answers will vary, as in the written CLAS assessments, they are either right or wrong, as in standardized tests. The grey areas come in degree of skill. For example, you give a second grader a bag of coins and ask her to show you $1.37. Depending on what coins could be in the bag, over 100 different coin combinations are possible. The answer is either right or wrong. Some students would be able to show the amount in a number of different ways. Some will miss it by $.01 when they are using lots of pennies. Some will do the task rapidly. Others will take a long time. These are the aforementioned degrees of skill and rubrics are easily developed which can measure them (Black 1997, 65–70).

The bottom line is still, "Can the student accurately count money or not?" Authentic assessments are in no way affected by reading comprehension or test-taking strategies. Students like authentic assessments because they can see the relevance and feel accomplishment. They're actually *doing* something, not "bubbling in" answers.

The most crucial portion of the assessment component is the pre-assessment. We cannot possibly know whether our teaching strategies are working if we are unaware whether students already had the requisite knowledge and skills *before* we began working with them. There is absolutely no point in wasting time teaching people what they already know.

Imagine you are supposed to teach swimming to a group of kids and fifty have signed up. What's the first thing you do? Get them in the water and see who can't float and who can already swim the length of the pool. In other words, you *assess what they already know and can do.*

Pre-assessment is a no-brainer. It is also a cutting edge concept in public education. Many teachers, particularly those focused on covering curriculum, do not know what to do with students who already know something. Some districts try to implement pre-assessment, but don't quite know how. A few are successful. More haven't even thought of it. Try this experiment: Sit in on a university course for teacher credentialing or educational administration. Wait for the instructor to pre-assess what the students already know. Warning: Please don't hold your breath. Why?

Think about it. When we're "covering curriculum," we don't *need* to know what students already know because to us it's irrelevant! Our units and lessons are already planned whether students have "been there, done that" or not. Whether they are ready or not. Whether they care or not. All they have to do is be quiet and pay attention and we'll talk about the stuff they're expected to know. *Voila!* Curriculum in a box. Prepackaged. Standardized. Conveyed. Bor-ing.

Customization

In the discussion of class size in Chapter 3, we saw that optimal size depends on

- the subject matter

- the strength of the teacher
- the ability level(s) of the students

Just as alternative medicine tends to customize treatments to wholistically fit each individual patient's needs and lifestyle, so an alternative education system should be able to do the same for students. It should do so not only in terms of class size, but learning modality as well.

Customization is not tracking. When kids want to learn to swim, to surf, to play the piano, to play basketball, we don't put them all in a sewing class and then congratulate ourselves on having eliminated tracking! There is nothing wrong with all kinds of groupings and purposes. What is wrong is our system with no real accountability and a license to be the only official game in town.

Focus on the Top, Not the Middle

In swimming, once you've determined who can't float and who's ready for the high dive, you divide up your groups for separate lessons. You'd never put someone who can't yet float in a class with someone who can swim laps. Need defines placement, not chronological age or grade. A ballet instructor would not place the new beginner in a class that's on point just because she's the same age as those students. The ski instructor does not group those learning to snowplow with those practicing moguls.

We not only do that in public education, we make them work together and call it "good for" both of them. In other words, we sacrifice the needs of the highest and the lowest and "teach to the middle." To the point near equilibrium, near center, the point to which we must always return, by design, in a closed system. In Chapter 6, we discussed reasons for focusing on the positive, on perfection, on "wellness" and on high standards in an alternative, open system.

Incentives and Advancement

One principal actually said to me, "I don't believe in tying teacher evaluation to student achievement." Then to what, pray tell, should we logically connect it? Can teachers logically be considered to be doing their jobs if students are not learning? But logic fails in our current system because there are too many constraints on teachers for them to be held accountable.

Not all students can reach the top. No matter how much legislators want to mandate that everyone be "above average," it's a mathematical impossibility. (Can you say "oxy-moronic"?) If a particular group is underachieving, financial or other state or federally supported incentives could help focus attention and assistance. A favorite argument against incentives is that everyone will want to teach the gifted. But, the gifted, as we saw in Chapter 6, are not automatically easy to teach. In fact, they are every bit as challenging as other students when properly taught. In addition, it can be harder to get from the 90th percentile to the 95th than from the 30th to the 35th.

Remember, with preassessment in place, it's possible for teacher, students and others to tell which teachers produce the greater percentages of gain in student achievement. Still, once again, incentives in the form of pay or advancement (possible in an alternative system) can help attract teachers to students who need them. Incentives are far more palatable when teachers have autonomy and the ability to advance (and a place to go!) based on the reputation and achievement they and their students build together.

Apprenticeship: Application and Transference

Apprenticeships and other application opportunities offer specialization and in-depth instruction in primary focus areas. Two or three hours per night and six to eight hours on weekends is commonplace for international competition level preparation in sports and for the arts. That's at least sixteen hours per week in one specialty area for kids between the ages of 14 and 18.

High schools have moved away from specialization because some students got "tracked" for unethical reasons. Rather than improve ethics, we chose to throw the baby out with the bathwater and delete developmental and career grouping. Recently we have begun coming back to the concept of specialization under new names like "career path."

Successful students still spend a lot of time on school and extracurricular pursuits and a lot on homework, but we do not support and encourage our best students the way coaches prepare theirs. We do not move from general studies into mastery, nor give them more one-on-one time, nor apprentice them to an expert. We could.

Apprenticeships are one method of helping students *apply* what they have learned in real situations and to transfer concepts among situations. "Real world" projects are another method. Authentic assessments can also begin the process of application. In each case, the student *applies* what she has learned to a real situation, often in a competitive format to get the adrenaline flowing. She places her skill and knowledge "on the line." She uses it, tests it, and comes away with a better understanding of where her strengths and weaknesses are and how her skills and knowledge compare with others'. She comes away knowing how much she's grown and where she needs to grow. She comes away ready to go back to work and knowing what to practice and why it needs practice.

Well, don't we have standardized tests for that same type of feedback? Goodness no! Standardized tests don't give us the same information because they don't test our ability to work in any real way in the world or even in a subject area. What do they test? They test our ability to read and comprehend English, to strategize about the intent of the test maker ("What answer do they want you to pick?"), to work quickly and under pressure. They test our recall and problem solving skills in English and math and sometimes other subject areas.

The results normally get to us in the fall of the year following the spring we took the test—a turnaround time that makes them virtually useless in instructional terms, but fairly useful in making us feel either inflated or defeated. Because they test what we were "supposed to learn" the previous year, not the curriculum for the current year, they do not serve as a valid pre-assessment, but rather like the swim coach asking new students to shoot hoops so she can determine which swim group to place them in.

Areas which afford us some flexible starting guidelines for our alternative design components include:

- apprenticeships
- customized curriculum ("differentiated instruction")
- focus at the top
- standards
- ongoing authentic pre- and post-assessments
- teacher incentives
- student interest

Using tools like the Internet, alternative programs will be able to network and support each other very rapidly and to develop their own, specialized components for success. Next we'll look at some other points to be considered in the context of our 21st century world.

9

21st Century Contextual Considerations

Education consists mainly in what we have unlearned.
—MARK TWAIN (Schiller 1999)

P aul Hawken, Amory Lovins and L. Hunter Lovins tackle the creation of open, living systems designs for 21st century business in their 1999 work, *Natural Capitalism*. What factors necessitate new designs so different from the old?

Overpopulation

Through the rise and establishment of capitalism, human resources were in low supply and natural resources appeared unlimited. Therefore, the capitalistic system design focused on efficiency and productivity in scarce human resources and the "inevitability" of waste in the use of our "unlimited" supply of natural resources. By then humans had no natural predators except fellow humans, which we could not control by using our brains. The Industrial Revolution added increases in prosperity and in food production. The Age of Reason with its new scientific worldview increased our sense of self-importance as lords and masters of a mechanical universe. Overpopulation was the result.

For over 200,000 years human population had remained relatively stable, barely doubling in all that time. Then, in a mere 300 years from the dawn to the end of the Industrial Age—between the mid-1600s and mid-1900s—human population quadrupled. At the same time, massive numbers of natural resources became endangered or extinct.

What's changed today is what's scarce. It's now the reverse of what our closed systems were designed for. Lovins, Lovins and Hawken call for a new capital system design, one that is in line with our overabundant supply of human labor and our endangered supply of planetary resources. They cite businesses already operating from the new systems designs, or what they term *natural capitalism*.

The point is simply that there is a parallel between business and education where the context in which the system was designed has reversed itself. In business, what was scarce and what was abundant changed places. In education, our design was based on uniformity and the need to educate only a few (males) beyond 8th grade or high school. We now have the most diverse and the most extensive student population on earth. We now have a square peg for a round hole. Our system's design cannot serve everyone.

Muda

A concept introduced by Toyota Production System creator, Taiichi Ohno, and defined as "any human activity which absorbs resources but creates no value" [Hawken, Lovins and Lovins 1999, 125], *muda* is, quite simply, waste. Americans represent 5% of the world's population, but consume some 30% of the world's resources. In production and consumption we generate enormous amounts of waste. "The total annual flow of waste in the American industrial system is 250 trillion pounds" (25×10^{13}) and "the total U.S. power plant heat waste equals Japan's total energy use" (Lovins and Lovins 1999). We generate much of this waste out of ignorance. We never faced the fact of finite resources.

We also never thought about where all the waste would go. Water is water is water. The water you drink today is the same water Moses parted. It's either in the air or on the ground or under the ground. Doesn't go anywhere, just changes form and recycles. We breathe the same air Confucius and Caesar did, as well as all land animals. The same air that trees recycle for us in their long lives. We tend to forget these simple facts when we pollute the water and air with our waste products. Businesses now using alternative practices as described by Hawkins *et al* are astoundingly more efficient and may actually serve to clean the air and water they use. *And* they are saving large amounts of money in the process.

In education, of course, waste takes human form: students we cannot or do not serve, people who get excluded from societal roles because they are too slow, too kinesthetic, too bright, too poor, too abused or too non-white to pass easily along our lock-stepped, graded conveyor belt. As in any assembly line, we still reject those who don't come out in standardized form. When our system was designed, dropouts could still make their way in the world quite successfully. Today, that is no longer true. The human cost of the rejection from our educational assembly line is high. Where do we think kids go when the system rejects them? How does our rejecting kids pollute our communities?

"I want that kid out of my class!" Out of the school, off the planet, far away. "He's disruptive! He's defiant! He's behind! He doesn't do any work! I can't teach with him in here! The class is fine when he's gone!" It's all true and it's definitely a problem. *He* is a problem. For him, *life* is a problem. He needs an attitude adjustment. He's got some learning difficulties. His mother was (pick a couple):

a) drinking
b) snorting
c) not eating
d) without medical care
e) being beaten
f) uneducated

when she was carrying him fifteen years ago.

He's either hyper or asleep (meaning he does ecstasy weekly at raves). He's in a crew or being jumped into a gang. Maybe he's already in a gang. He reads English at a third grade level and doesn't know his multiplication tables. We want him out of the classroom. (Yes, but to where?) He can't sit quietly at a desk for 45 minutes and take notes on what we tell him were the causes of the Civil War without bothering other students or interrupting us.

We're covering curriculum. Of course he's disruptive! Of course he's defiant! But do we really want him on the streets with nothing to do all day except hang around outside our houses? Are we really ready to consign him to jail at 14? That's where he's headed. Does it seem so farfetched to create alternative educational systems designs that might better address the needs of non-standardized students like him? Still not convinced? Let's give him a face.

A young man sits in front of my desk slouched low in the chair, hands in his pockets, feet sprawled, head cocked to one side, jaw set. He has enormous brown eyes, a slow, crooked smile, and ears he terms "big" which make him self-conscious. He faces me and sits up respectfully as I begin to address him, "Hey, what happened?" I can see the pain in his face. I get up from my chair and round the desk to sit on the chair next to his. His jaws clench, muscles twitching. His eyes are moist. He leans forward, hands dangling helplessly between his knees, and turns his head away, looking down. We talk quietly.

We've had many conversations over the past year. We've discussed his schoolwork, his home life, his girlfriend, his single inch-long fingernail (which he's since cut, hopefully because he's using something less dangerous now). I have gone to bat for him on a number of occasions, which has caused me grief from the staff. And he knows it. He has done everything I've ever asked him to try. And I know what my requests have cost him in terms of pride and self-control. There is mutual respect here and a level of trust, which it is now my job description to shatter.

He has just called one of his teachers a "fuckin' bitch." Obviously it isn't the first time he's been in my office for offenses of similar severity. But it will be the last. This suspension, added to the others, will place him at the top of the list of students being transferred to the district's alternative program. For some, the program works. For many, it's another step down the staircase. But, he'll be out of that teacher's classroom. The staff individually congratulate me following my confidential memo that he is withdrawing. He will no longer disrupt their classes or school activities. He'll be off our campus. Out of sight, out of mind. I go home and consider resigning.

The alternative program welcomes him when I accompany him and his mother to the intake interview. The Director comments that the boy should feel special because I don't come to every intake. I think to myself, "I should." I have a real investment in this kid, having tried so hard to prevent the need for this placement. I leave my card with the boy and his mother. Out of sight, out of mind. Not mine.

Three weeks pass and I see the Director at a meeting. We pause to update each other and I ask about "my kid." Last I'd heard, he'd done well the first two weeks at the new school. Yes, he had. Then last week he brought an illegal item to school and was expelled from the district.

I phone his house to see how he's doing. His mother is distraught. He hasn't been home for three days. She knows I've already done a lot for him, but is there something I can do now? I phone the police. The boy returns home. The gang task force officer makes another home visit, tries to reason with the boy and tell his mother what trouble signs to look for at home. His mother and I get him enrolled at the county alternative school. Summer comes and I see him only once.

The following fall I'm called from my office by a campus supervisor an hour after school because six high-school-aged boys are hanging around our middle school campus and refusing to leave for her or for the custodian. Ok. I'm sure all six of them are going to listen to all 5'4" of me.

Opening my cell phone, prepared to call the police, I cross the field to the picnic table where the boys are sitting. I note the biggest one, about 5'11" and 200 pounds, and obviously no longer a student anywhere. I don't know him or the one sitting across from him. I approach and turn to look at the rest of the group. There he is.

We laugh and do the handshake he taught me. We kid around and make small talk. The boys get up and head out agreeably for me. He and I hang behind the others as we walk back across the field. I quietly let him know that his jacket smells like what he's been smoking and that he might want to take it off if he were to see the police anywhere because it puts him in violation of his probation. He begins to tell me he doesn't know what I'm talking about, catches my look, and grins, "Okay, Ms. Black." We say goodbye. I go in and call the police.

I'm alone when my desk clock reads 5 P.M. and tears come. I

know it was a gang meeting that I broke up. He has a new home now. This is human *muda*.

Who failed this boy? Me? His teachers? His parents? His church? His community? Yes, of course. But, his teachers and I would have stood a better chance were we not working in a system that threw "irregulars" off the conveyor belt. Waste isn't natural. Recycling *is*. We desperately need an alternative system where kids like this can learn something other than how to tag or how to knife an opposing gang member. Where they can fit. Where they could flourish.

Conclusion

It is not easy to be a pioneer—but oh, it is fascinating! I would not trade one moment, even the worst moment, for all the riches in the world.
    —ELIZABETH BLACKWELL (Zadra and Carlson 1995)

I have a friend who works as a professional rafting guide during the summers. He's quite good at it. He proudly informed a group of us that he normally does not take the same route all the other guides take, but likes to find his own path through the current. Those of us in his raft had a lot of fun! The jokes were hilarious; our ride was tremendously exciting and no one went overboard.

Like I said, he's good at it.

He's good at it when he follows his own path. When he is forced to follow along behind other rafts, he decreases to just above average. Where would we be if Beethoven had been forced to write like Mozart? If Mother Teresa had been told "No" she could not do her work? And had listened? If Thomas Jefferson had written the Declaration of *Reform*?

The same route doesn't work for everyone.

We don't all learn alike, think alike, relate to the same things. Intelligent, creative people *need* to do things in their own way. People with special needs, different learning modalities and creative teaching styles do, too. There is no formula, no map, no "new size" for all. There are simply alternatives, and we need to be willing to let people try them.

Clearly, I am like my friend: I prefer finding my own path. And, like him, when I'm not constricted by my position or by generalized regulations, the results are more than satisfactory for me and for those "rafting" with me. So, how will I do that? What's my path?

Right now I see charter schools as the best door out of The Box. They do not eschew the current public system but work alongside it as an alternative for those of us who need a different route. While I have been writing this book and working full-time during the past four years, I have been "in development" on a charter school, to borrow a phrase from my days at MGM/UA. In a few days, when I FedEx a disk of the final draft to my editor, I will move into pre-production on the charter.

My colleagues and I will create a projects-based apprenticeship program around the arts and deep ecology for students whose high I.Q., street smarts and/or deviant behavior creates a severe mismatch with the traditional classroom. Students like the ones in Chapters 6 and 9.

We will follow the same state curriculum frameworks. We will use the same standardized tests, as well as many authentic pre- and post- and ongoing assessments. Our students will prepare for California's High School Exit Exam (HSEE). We will reach the same goals along a more personalized path. We will probably all work harder—students and staff—than we did in traditional public schools. But work we love feels more like play, while work that seems pointless or imposed can feel like drudgery.

Love of learning is natural. That there is more than one way to learn is natural, too. If we are to truly educate a diverse public, we must diversify education—and not just once per unit nor once a week, nor even once an hour. *We're* more diverse than that. Our education must be, too.

Not everyone will want to find their own route through the current. There is no need. They can continue to work in the current structures, alongside our new alternative systems. Their reticence doesn't make them wrong, nor others wrong for trying a new way. What we didn't know or understand about our public education system has hurt us and our future. At least some of us need to find a way out of The Box, a new route, our own path through the current. It is time to stop complaining about and trying to "reform" public education. It's time to let everyone have the chance to learn and teach in their own way. And be good at it.

References

Baum, L. Frank. 1987. *The Wonderful Wizard of Oz.* New York: William Morrow.

Black, Caren. 1997. *Getting Out of Line.* Thousand Oaks, CA: Corwin.

Bracey, Gerald W. 1997. *Setting the Record Straight.* Alexandria, VA: Association for Supervision and Curriculum Development.

CSR Research Consortium. June 2000. *Summary of the 1998–1999 Evaluation Findings.* Sacramento: California Department of Education.

Capra, Fritjof. 1996. *The Web of Life.* New York: Anchor Doubleday.

Casteneda, Carlos. 1968. *Conversations with Don Juan: A Yaqui Way of Knowledge.* New York: Pocket Books.

Dannis, Gregory J. 1999. "An Exclusive Interview with California K–12 Education." Keynote address at the annual Miller Brown and Dannis Workshop, San Francisco.

EdSource. 1997–1998. *Resource Cards.* Palo Alto. CA: EdSource.

———. February 1998. "Evaluating California's Class Size Reduction Program." Palo Alto, CA: EdSource.

———. April 1998. "California's School Facilities Predicament." Palo Alto, CA: EdSource.

———. November 1998. "How California Compares." Palo Alto, CA: EdSource.

Gatto, John Taylor. 1995. "A Different Kind of Teacher." *Gateway* 5: 1–13.

Gilroy Unified School District. 2000–2001 budget. Gilroy, California.

Hawken, Paul, Amory Lovins, and L. Hunter Lovins. 1999. *Natural Capitalism.* Boston: Little, Brown.

Krovetz, Martin. 1999. *Fostering Resiliency: Expecting All Students to Use Their Minds and Hearts Well.* Thousand Oaks, CA: Corwin.

Land, George, and Beth Jarman. 1992. *Breakpoint and Beyond.* New York: HarperBusiness.

Lovins, Amory, and L. Hunter Lovins. 1999. Keynote address at Bioneers Conference, 30 October, Marin, California.

Molnar, Alex. 2000. *Vouchers, Class Size Reduction, and Student Achievement.* Bloomington, IN: Phi Delta Kappa.

National Campaign to Prevent Teen Pregnancy. 28 July 2000. *Facts and Stats.* <http://www.teenpregnancy.org/genlfact.htm>

National Center for Education Statistics. 1999. "Elementary and Secondary Education." Chapter 2 of *Digest of Education Statistics.* <http://nces.ed.gov/pubs2000/digest99/>

Patterson, Martha. 2000. Research questionnaire.

Ravitch, Diane. 2000. *Left Back: A Century of Failed School Reforms.* New York: Simon and Schuster.

Saxe, John Godfrey. "The Blind Men and the Elephant." <http://www.noogenesis.com/pineapple/blind_men_elephant.html>

Schaef, Anne Wilson, and Diane Fassel. 1988. *The Addictive Organization.* San Francisco: Harper and Row.

Schapiro, Dennis, and Brenda Hellen, eds. 1998. *Montessori Community Resource.* Minneapolis, MN: Jola Publications.

Schiller, David. 1999. *Little Zen Calendar.* New York: Workman.

Spring, Joel. 1989. *American Education.* New York: Longman.

von Bertalanffy, Ludwig. 1968. *General System Theory.* New York: Braziller.

Wallis, Claudia. 1991. "Why New Age Medicine Is Catching On." *Time Magazine* 4 November: 68.

WestEd. 22 July 1996. *The Devil Is in the Details: New Funds for Class-Size Reduction.* <http://www.wested.org/policy/hot_top/csr/ht_tp _maynov96.htm>

Winokur, Jon. 1989. *Zen to Go.* New York: New American Library.

Zadra, Dan, with Susan Carlson. 1995. *Brilliance: Uncommon Voices from Uncommon Women,* Edmonds, WA: Compendium.

Index